XENOPHON
THE FALL OF ATHENS

XENOPHON
THE FALL OF ATHENS
SELECTIONS FROM THE HELLENICA OF XENOPHON

EDITED WITH INTRODUCTION
AND VOCABULARY
BY THEODORE HORN, MA

PUBLISHED BY BRISTOL CLASSICAL PRESS
GENERAL EDITOR: JOHN H. BETTS
(BY ARRANGEMENT WITH MACMILLAN & CO. LTD)

Cover illustration: Horse's head from the chariot of Selene on the east
pediment of the Parthenon. Fifth century; British Museum, London.

First published in 1962 by Macmillan & Co. Ltd

New edition published in 1978 by
Bristol Classical Press
an imprint of
Gerald Duckworth & Co. Ltd
The Old Piano Factory
48 Hoxton Square, London N1 6PB

Reprinted 1990, 1992, 1993, 1995

A catalogue record for this book is available
from the British Library

ISBN 0-906515-12-2

Available in USA and Canada from:
Focus Information Group
PO Box 369
Newburyport
MA 01950

Printed in Great Britain by
Booksprint, Bristol

CONTENTS

LIST OF MAPS AND ILLUSTRATIONS

ACKNOWLEDGMENT

The frontispiece and the illustrations on pages xii, xxiv, 13 and 27 have been reproduced from *Greece in Photographs* by kind permission of Messrs. Thames and Hudson.

LIST OF SELECTIONS AND REFERENCES

PREFACE TO THE FIRST EDITION

So far as I know there has been no school edition of these exciting chapters of Xenophon's *Hellenica* since the edition of Hailstone (Macmillan, 1878) and Edwards (Cambridge, 1899), though both have been reprinted many times. I have selected passages which give the main events of the years 410-404 BC, having in mind sufficient reading for a term at Ordinary Level of the G.C.E.

The text is Hailstone's, with certain modifications in spelling, particularly in proper names. I have not discussed the text in detail, but I have referred to doubtful readings in certain passages. It does no harm for even young pupils to realise some of the problems raised by the transmission of ancient books through many centuries.

For the notes, I have given such help as I should expect to be useful at this stage, in grammar explaining difficult or unusual constructions and in translation suggesting a version where this may be helpful. In the subject matter I have tried to show that we are dealing with real people who had to face actual problems, some of which are still with us – the difficulty of reconciling the conflicting claims of allies, interference by an outside power in the internal affairs of state, and party strife based on what is now termed ideology. It is interesting also to consider how ships and men were handled, and what conditions of active service were like in ancient times.

I have consulted the editions named above and the *Oxford Classical Text of Xenophon*, and Goodwin in particular for points of grammar. For the history, Grote (who is still first-rate reading), Bury, the *Cambridge Ancient History*, and notes taken many years ago in the lecture rooms of Oxford. The *Oxford Classical Dictionary* I have found most helpful. I owe an incalculable debt to my schoolmasters and tutors, and to friends and colleagues for much interest and advice. I owe also something to certain boys at Stockport Grammar School, who perhaps taught me almost as much as I taught them. And I should like to pay a tribute to my former tutor in Ancient History, the late Dr B.W. Henderson, whose incisive criticisms and profound historical sense I used to find both humbling and inspiring.

My thanks are also due to the unfailing helpfulness and courtesy shown by the staff of Messrs. Macmillan.

T.H.
Stockport
December, 1960

PREFACE TO BRISTOL CLASSICAL PRESS EDITION

This new edition is published as a result of the kind co-operation of Macmillan Educational. The editor also owes a debt of gratitude to Mrs M. Nicol of King Edward VI High School for Girls, Birmingham; and to Mr D.J.D. Miller of the Bristol Grammar School, who kindly supplied the following *errata* to the first edition:

p. 4 1. 57   read τῶν for τῷν
p. 4 1. 62   read μηνοῖν for μγνοῖν
p. 18 1. 34   read διεσκεδασμέναι for διεσκδασμέναι
p. 20 1. 6   read 'Αριστοκράτους for Αριστοκράτους
p. 27 1. 3   read τειχῶν for πειχῶν
p. 30 1. 44   read πεμφθεὶς for πεμφεὶς
p. 66   add πρῷρα, τά, prow, bows

J.H.B.
Bristol
December 1977

INTRODUCTION

Section 1. Xenophon and his Works

Xenophon is a most interesting personality. At once a man of action, a man of affairs, and a man of letters, he represents the Greek ideal of manly excellence, a body and a mind alike well trained and developed, and a capacity to perform the duties of a citizen both in peace and in war.

The son of Gryllus, an Athenian of the deme of Erchia, he was born about 431 B.C. He was thus a boy during the early years of the Peloponnesian War, but by the time of the Sicilian Expedition (415–413 B.C.) he would be almost old enough to be called up for military service; as he seems to have served in the cavalry his family would be wealthy, for members of the cavalry provided their own horses. We do not know what service he saw. Cavalry played a very small part in Greek warfare, and Attica itself is not good country for cavalry operations. His service may have amounted to little beyond patrolling, but two of his books show not only his interest but also his competence. In later life he was to write two valuable treatises, one, the *Hipparchus*, on the duties of a cavalry commander, and the other, *On horsemanship*, a complete manual on the subject.

Another influence in these early years was his association with Socrates. Like many another young Athenian he was greatly attracted by that remarkable man, and though apparently never one of the inner circle of pupils, he saw enough of him to write later the

Memorabilia, somewhat discursive recollections, and an *Apology*, the object of which was to show how Socrates could have defended himself more successfully.

In 401 B.C. began the great experience of Xenophon's life. He was invited by his friend Proxenus of Thebes to accompany a force of mercenary Greek soldiers in an expedition under Cyrus the Younger. The real object of this was not at first disclosed, but the force found itself committed to an invasion of Persia in an attempt to dethrone King Artaxerxes, the brother of Cyrus. In the *Anabasis*, his best known work, Xenophon describes the adventure; the march up country from Sardis, the victory at the Battle of Cunaxa, the death of Cyrus and the subsequent dispersal of his army, the treacherous murder of the Greek generals, and the amazing enterprise of the Greeks. For with superb initiative and courage, isolated in Mesopotamia, this small force of ten thousand Greeks elected new generals and marched and fought their way up the Tigris valley and across the mountains of Armenia till they reached the Greek colony of Trapezus on the shores of the Black Sea, after suffering incredible hardships through snow, hunger, and the hostility of the natives. It is clear that Xenophon himself showed great qualities of personality and leadership; his own account, though written some years later, is full of fresh and vigorous writing. The scene where the weary Greeks top the last ridge and at last catch sight of the sea is one of the most dramatic in ancient literature.

After further vicissitudes Xenophon handed over the remnants of the mercenaries of Cyrus to the Spartan commander at the Hellespont, and himself seems to have

taken service under the Spartans. In 399 B.C. a decree
of banishment was passed against him at Athens. The
exact charge is not known, but it may well have been the
fact that he had served under Cyrus and with the
Spartans. He had married a certain Philesia, and by
394 B.C. his two sons, Gryllus and Diodorus, were old
enough to be educated at Sparta. Xenophon was a
close friend of King Agesilaus, of whom he wrote an
admiring memoir, and was present with him at the
battle of Coronea in 394 B.C. The Spartan government
gave him an estate at Scillus, near Olympia, where he
settled and devoted himself to writing, the management
of his estate, and the pursuits of a country gentleman.
One of his works is the *Oeconomicus*, a dialogue on estate
management, which, if not autobiographical, certainly
gives a charming picture of the family life, pursuits, and
pleasures which Xenophon himself must have enjoyed.
It is to be noted that among these he included the
worship and service of the gods.

Xenophon wrote in all fourteen books, of which the
Anabasis and the *Hellenica* are the most valuable. It is
not known when he wrote the *Hellenica*. The division
into seven books is certainly not due to Xenophon
himself, but there is a distinct break after Book II.
The first two books continue the story of the Peloponnesian War from the point where Thucydides breaks off
in 411 B.C. to the downfall of the Thirty Tyrants and the
restoration of the Athenian democracy in 403 B.C.
These two books may well have been written early.
The later books end with the Battle of Mantinea in
362 B.C., and the work was unfinished in 358 B.C.
Annalistic in form and with some omissions and much

ATHENS: THE AGORA
Excavations in progress

bias, the *Hellenica* is yet a valuable contribution to Greek history. Another interesting work is the *Cyropaedia*, an idealized biography of Cyrus the Elder. Partly it gives an account of principles of education which Xenophon elsewhere ascribes to Socrates, and partly it embodies Xenophon's ideal of the good ruler.

In 371 B.C., when Elis recovered Scillus from Sparta, Xenophon lost his estate and moved to Corinth. About 369 B.C. his sentence of banishment was revoked and he was able to return to Athens, though he seems to have made his residence at Corinth. His sons took service in the Athenian cavalry, and the elder, Gryllus, fell in action at the Battle of Mantinea. A pamphlet of Xenophon's on the finances of Athens appears to be dated about 355 B.C. This may well have been his last work, for he is believed to have died in Corinth, in or shortly after 354 B.C.

SECTION 2. HISTORICAL PRELUDE

The Peloponnesian War, the great war between Athens and Sparta, lasted for twenty-seven years, from 431 to 404 B.C. For the first twenty years our main authority is the incomparable *History* of Thucydides, who himself served as general in the early years. His work breaks off in the autumn of 411 B.C., and in the first two books of the *Hellenica* Xenophon continues the narrative to the final defeat of Athens in 404 B.C., the rise and fall of the Thirty Tyrants, and the restoration of the democracy eighteen months later.

Briefly, the causes of the war were that Sparta was jealous of and feared Athenian supremacy in Greece, certain allies of Athens, members of the Delian League, feared the loss of their independence, and Corinth felt a constant threat to her commerce. The outbreak of war was hastened by three incidents. Corinth had a dispute with her colony, Corcyra, and Corcyra appealed to Athens. An alliance was made (433 B.C.), and Corinth was worsted. In Thrace, another Corinthian colony, Potidaea, a member of the Delian League, revolted, and was besieged by an Athenian force. Potidaea appealed both to Corinth and to Sparta. Finally, in the same year, 432 B.C., Athens took the step of imposing economic sanctions on Megara by passing the decree which excluded the Megarians from the markets of Attica and harbours of the Athenian Empire. Athens had grievances against Megara, but this decree was really designed to give warning to all of the formidable power she possessed.

Athens was strong mainly at sea, Sparta and her allies by land. Athens could send what is now called a task force anywhere she chose; Sparta could and did regularly invade and harry Attica, but was powerless to attack Athens itself and the Piraeus, which were joined and defended by the Long Walls. Thucydides comments that both sides increasingly showed great cruelty, and bitter party strife, amounting often to civil war, was an unpleasant occurrence in many cities. During the course of the war few Greek states were not at some time involved, and the battlefield was the whole of the Greek world.

In the first ten years of the war there were operations in north-west Greece, in Boeotia (where Plataea was besieged and captured, Athens thus losing a loyal ally), at Pylos and Sphacteria on the west coast of the Peloponnese (425 and 424 B.C.), in Boeotia again in 424 B.C., and in Thrace, where the Spartan general Brasidas was brilliantly successful until his untimely death. Athens faced two serious crises; a devasting outbreak of the plague in the overcrowded city, and the first revolt of any of her allies, Mytilene. The death of Pericles by plague deprived Athens of a wise and consistent leader. There was no-one of the same calibre to take his place, and there came to the front a number of popular leaders, men such as Cleon and Hyperbolus, of low birth and little wisdom, who possessed the power of swaying the Assembly by their violent harangues. It is significant that these demagogues, leaders of the popular party, were strenuous in advocating an imperialistic and aggressive policy, and the revolt of Mitylene was savagely crushed. In 421 B.C. the short-lived Peace of Nicias was negotiated.

When this peace was soon broken, there followed a campaign in the Peloponnese which the Spartans brought to an end by their victory at Mantinea in 418 B.C. Athens continued to treat her allies and dependents with increasing tyranny, and in 417 B.C. the small island of Melos was wantonly attacked and enslaved; she was determined to keep her grip on the Aegean. Then, in 415 B.C., she launched the most spectacular and ambitious enterprise of the war, the Sicilian Expedition. The object was to capture Syracuse, assert supremacy over the Greek cities of the West, and secure their resources for herself. After nearly two years of frustrated effort, the attack on Syracuse failed, and the Athenian armament was destroyed.

This failure had dire results for Athens. Apart from the terrible blow to her prestige, she had lost many ships and irreplaceable men, her treasury was exhausted, the West was now closed to her, and her allies were beginning to revolt. She depended on imported supplies, particularly from the Aegean and the Euxine.

If she lost control of these trade routes, defeat was inevitable. Hence the last stages of the war are set in the Aegean and the Propontis. Here also Persia was prepared to take a hand, and Sparta had no scruples in making an ally of the traditional enemy.

Another result was dissatisfaction with the form of government in Athens, not only on the part of those who had always hated the democracy, but also in the minds of more moderate men. The democracy had shown its weakness by hasty and unwise decisions; it had appointed an unsuitable commander for the Sicilian expedition, Nicias, and had recalled and exiled Alcibiades; its administration was unsatisfactory. As a preliminary, ten commissioners, called Probuli, were appointed to examine the situation. A cumbersome scheme based on a responsible body of five thousand citizens only was drawn up, but never came into force, and a council of four hundred was ultimately charged with the duties of government. It was nominally a provisional arrangement, but the controlling power in the Four Hundred was in the hands of the oligarchic party, and during the summer of 411 B.C. they acted as a dictatorship. They could do this largely because most of the supporters of the democracy were absent with the fleet which had its headquarters at Samos. Discontent with the Four Hundred was brought to a head by the revolt and loss of Euboea. A meeting of the Ecclesia was held at Samos, the movement spread to Athens, where another meeting of the Ecclesia deposed the Four Hundred, and a modified democracy was set up, mainly under the influence of Theramenes.

The Ecclesia at Samos had recalled Alcibiades and

elected new generals, of whom he was one. He opened negotiations with the Persian satrap, but failed to cause a break between Sparta and Persia. The year 411 B.C. closed with Athenian successes at Cynossema and Abydos, and at that point the narrative of Xenophon begins.

A note may be added on the position of Persia. The Western part of Asia Minor was administered as two satrapies or provinces; the satrap of Sardis was Tissaphernes, of Phrygia, Pharnabazus. Their object was to take advantage of the weakness of Athens to restore to Persian sovereignty those cities in Asia which were Athenian allies or subjects. In return, they were prepared to replenish the impoverished treasury of Sparta by contributing to the cost of her fleet. The alliance concluded by Sparta with Persia did not pass without protest in Greece, but the days when 'medism' was a crime had passed. It seemed more important to settle the long quarrel with Athens and humble her for ever.

SECTION 3. SOME OF THE PERSONALITIES

Before we look at some of the personalities of these closing years of the Peloponnesian War, it may be helpful to consider some of the political terms and institutions involved.

In Greek history we constantly come across the words 'oligarch' and 'democrat'. Oligarchy means government by a minority, usually a small, exclusive class, relying on birth, wealth, or position. Such was the government of Venice in the Middle Ages. In a democracy on the other hand, supreme power rested with the citizen body as a whole, acting either through elected magistrates or directly by discussion and vote in an assembly. Greek states were small and it was possible for all the citizens to meet as a body. The terms 'oligarch' and 'democrat' are used not only for those who in a given case are in power, but also for the political parties which support a particular form of government. Party strife was a common feature of Greek political life, and during the Peloponnesian War it became a curse. Thucydides comments strongly on this, and his account of party strife in Corcyra and other states makes terrible reading. Intense political strife has also been a characteristic of modern Greece.

The most important office in Athens was that of 'general', $\sigma\tau\rho\alpha\tau\eta\gamma\delta\varsigma$. It is convenient to keep this translation, but it must be remembered that it means 'a commander in the armed forces'. As in the Royal Navy in the seventeenth century, when a general might be in command of the fleet, a 'general' was expected to command by land or sea as the situation required. Even when all other offices of state were filled by the casting of lots, the office of general remained elective. It thus depended on and involved some political influence, but it is only fair to say that some excellent choices were often made.

Sparta, strange to say, though not a sea-power, had the rank of admiral, $\nu\alpha\nu\alpha\rho\chi\sigma\varsigma$ for those who commanded the fleets which were found mainly by her allies. Sparta again had a curious constitution, which comprised a dual, hereditary, kingship, a senate, and an assembly of citizens. It must be remembered that the Spartan citizens formed only a minority of the population. But the most curious feature was a board of five elected magistrates called ephors, ἔφοροι, who had wide powers of supervision and control. Thus they conducted negotiations with other states, saw to it that Spartan customs were duly observed, and, most remarkable of all, while one of the kings normally commanded the army in the field, two of them accompanied him to observe and check his conduct of the campaign.

Alcibiades

Alcibiades is one of the most remarkable characters in Greek history. Born in Athens about 450 B.C., on his mother's side he belonged to the famous family of the Alcmaeonidae. When his father Clinias was killed at the Battle of Coronea in 447 B.C., he became a ward of his relative Pericles, and was thus brought up in the atmosphere of democratic government. Of striking beauty and physique he showed from his earliest years strong passions and an ambitious personality. He became a constant associate of Socrates, with whom he saw military service in Thrace and at the Battle of Delium. Socrates endeavoured to influence the best qualities of his brilliant pupil, but flatterers played on his vanity and ambition, and his extravagance and licentiousness were notorious.

Nevertheless with birth, wealth, personal courage, and eloquence in his favour, he became prominent as a leader of the extreme democrats in opposition to the moderate party led by Nicias. It was Alcibiades who engineered the alliance with Argos and other Peloponnesian states in 420 B.C. This did not survive the Spartan victory at Mantinea in 418 B.C. But his aggressive aims led him strongly to support the Sicilian Expedition in 415 B.C. He was indeed sent out as one of the generals in command, and the result of this enterprise might have been very different had he not been recalled almost at once. He was recalled to stand trial on two counts. It was alleged that in his house in Athens he had celebrated a profane mockery of the Eleusinian mysteries, and that he was responsible for the mutilation of the Hermae. One night, just before the Sicilian Expedition sailed, the small figures of Hermes which stood before Athenian houses were found to have been wantonly damaged. Who perpetrated this act of desecration has never been established, but Alcibiades was blamed. He did not return to Athens, was promptly sentenced to banishment, and took refuge in Sparta.

In Sparta he did his own city as much harm as he could. On his advice the Spartan government sent a Spartan general to take command in Syracuse and occupied and fortified Decelea, a strategic position in Attica only some fifteen miles from Athens. Alcibiades adopted Spartan dress and habits, but he quarrelled with King Agis and departed for Ionia. Here he endeavoured to embroil Sparta and Persia and to obtain Persian aid for Athens. He then made overtures to the Athenian fleet at Samos, was elected general, and led their fleet to victory at Cyzicus.

After further successes he felt able to return to Athens. His exile was rescinded and he was appointed general in supreme command. But when he returned to Samos to take over the fleet he committed the folly of entrusting a part of it to a favourite of his, Antiochus, who was decisively defeated at Notium. This disaster, together with further complaints of his dissolute living, led to his withdrawal to a fortress which he owned in Thrace.

The last service he attempted to render Athens was to advise the Athenian commanders at Aegospotami to move to a safer anchorage, advice which was unwisely rejected. After the fall of Athens in 404 B.C., there were still hopes that he might yet save his city, and Lysander conspired with the Persian satrap Pharnabazus to make an end of him, and he was attacked and murdered in a village in Phrygia which he was visiting.

No man could have done more for Athens in her difficulties than Alcibiades. Yet in spite of his great abilities he was fundamentally unstable. His fellow-citizens did not trust him. His tragedy is that he hurt Athens as much as himself.

Conon

We know Conon only as a capable and enterprising naval officer; he seems to have taken no active part in politics. He was born about 444 B.C., and we first hear of him in 414 B.C. in command of an Athenian squadron at Naupactus, where he was stationed to try and prevent Corinthian reinforcements from sailing for Syracuse.

Seven years later (Autumn 407 B.C.), on the disgrace of Alcibiades, he was elected one of the ten generals and ordered to take over the fleet which Alcibiades had commanded. He found the fleet discouraged after the defeat at Notium and set to work to restore efficiency and morale.

In the summer of 406 B.C. he was defeated by a Peloponnesian fleet of superior numbers and blockaded

at Mitylene. He contrived to send news of his plight to
Athens, but was still blockaded when the battle of
Arginusae was fought. It is an interesting specula-
tion that his presence there might have prevented the
failure to rescue the drowning Athenian sailors, and
so the tragic trial of the generals might never have taken
place.

A year later, at Aegospotami, the Athenian fleet took
up a most unfavourable position. Possibly Conon was
overruled by his colleagues, as it seems hardly likely
that he would have chosen such a station or allowed
Lysander to bring off his surprise attack. He was at
least alert and his division of the fleet alone was ready
for action. He had no choice but to escape. Even so
he performed an act of great daring in crossing the
straits and seizing the sails of Lysander's ships which
had been deposited ashore at Cape Abarnis. Then he
sent the Paralus with the news to Athens, and himself
sailed to Cyprus, where he took service under Evagoras
the ruler of Salamis.

In 400 B.C. Sparta went to war with Persia. Through
the influence of Evagoras Conon was able to help the
Persians to revive their sea power, and in 397 B.C. he
was in command of their fleet. At Cnidus, in 394 B.C.,
he avenged Aegospotami by utterly defeating the
Spartan fleet. Returning to Athens, he helped with the
last stages in rebuilding the Long Walls, which restored
her self-respect. In 392 B.C. he was sent on a diplomatic
mission to Sardis, where he was arrested by the Persians.
He escaped, returned to Cyprus, and died shortly after.
It is a misfortune that we do not know more about this
brave and capable Athenian.

Theramenes

Theramenes is most commonly remembered for the nickname κόθορνος, given to him by his opponents of both parties. The cothurnus or buskin was the large boot worn by tragic actors on the Athenian stage; it could be worn on either foot, and Theramenes earned this nickname by his frequent change of party.

Born about 455 B.C., he was the son of Hagnon, who was chosen as one of the ten commissioners (πρόβουλοι) appointed in 413 B.C. to advise on constitutional changes and act as a temporary executive body. The family must have been wealthy, for Theramenes served a term as trierarch. He first became prominent in this political crisis which was accentuated by the revolt of the Athenian allies in 412 B.C. He was one of those who were gravely dissatisfied with the extreme democratic government and its conduct of the war. He thus strongly supported the proposed constitution of the Five Thousand, and when this proved abortive he became one of the oligarchy of the Four Hundred. When in turn this short-lived government fell (411 B.C.) he took a leading part in establishing a modified form of democracy, and he worked with Alcibiades to restore Athenian naval supremacy.

He was present at Arginusae in the capacity of trierarch. After the battle, the generals were brought to trial on the charge that they had culpably neglected to rescue the Athenian sailors still clinging to the water-logged vessels damaged in the action, in spite of their claim that a storm had suddenly blown up. Theramenes vigorously supported the accusation. The generals

ATHENS: VIEW FROM THE NORTH PORCH OF
THE TEMPLE OF ERECHTHEUS ON THE ACROPOLIS
looking over the Plain of the Cephisus

retorted that they had in fact given orders to Theramenes
himself and other trierarchs to carry out this task but
excused their failure to do so on account of the storm.
It is impossible now to decide how far any blame can be
allotted and to whom, but in spite of a glaring piece of
illegality in the proceedings, the six generals who had
faced their accusers were condemned and executed.

For this Theramenes must be held partly responsible.

In 404 B.C., when Athens realized that it was no longer possible to carry on the war, and harsh terms of peace were likely, Theramenes went personally to Lysander to obtain better terms. He remained absent from Athens for three months, no doubt to gain time. Finally he was sent to Sparta with full powers to make peace. When the democracy was replaced by a body of thirty to form and carry on the government, a body known as the Thirty Tyrants, Theramenes was one of those chosen. But he did not agree with their excesses of cruelty and political persecution, fell foul of their leader Critias and the other extremists, and was liquidated before the end of 404 B.C.

In ancient times Theramenes was censured for his frequent change of sides, both by oligarchs and democrats; he was defended as aiming at any possible form of government which should be stable and capable of coping with the situation. There is no reason to dismiss him as a self-seeking politician. He seems to have been one of those who paid the penalty of regarding stability and competence as of more importance in a government than rigid party principles.

Socrates

It is not possible here to give anything like a full note on Socrates. He appears once in the narrative covered by these selections, not as the philosopher diligently in search of truth or asking pertinent questions in order to make men think about the things in life that really matter or as the wise teacher of the youth of Athens, but as a citizen performing the duties required of him as the state directed and bravely refusing to act illegally in spite of the vehement demands of an angry Ecclesia. It so happened that at the trial of the generals in 406 B.C. Socrates was one of the presidents (πρυτάνεις) of the assembly. When it was demanded that the generals be judged and condemned together, contrary to established procedure, Socrates refused to put the motion.

That this was characteristic of him is shown by other acts in his life. He served as a hoplite in the army, and was commended for valour at the Battle of Delium in 424 B.C., when he was forty-five years old. After the peace of 404 B.C. Athens was for eighteen months ruled by an oligarchy called the Thirty Tyrants, whose actions in many ways resembled those of certain totalitarian governments of our time. They forbade intellectual and philosophical teaching, a decree with which Socrates refused to comply. And in a wave of indiscriminate arrests of their opponents, they insisted on blameless citizens carrying out these arrests in order to implicate them in their enormities. On one occasion five Athenians were ordered to arrest a certain Leon. Four of them carried out the order; the fifth, Socrates, refused. Such was the man who faced trial and condemnation in 399 B.C. and lives in the pages of Plato and Xenophon.

Lysander

'Some talk ... of Hector and Lysander', but in fact Lysander was as much a diplomat and politician as he was a soldier or sailor. Plutarch tells us that he came of a noble but impoverished family, remained poor, and was never corrupted by wealth. He was, however, ambitious and craved distinction.

When he was sent out as admiral to the eastern Aegean at the end of 408 or early in 407 B.C., Athens had temporarily regained her position. On his arrival he set to work to reorganize the Peloponnesian fleet and restore Spartan influence. His arrival coincided with the appointment of Cyrus as Persian governor in Asia Minor. From the start he won the confidence of Cyrus by his astute diplomacy and obtained enough money from him to raise the pay of his seamen, which helped to restore their morale. The trust Cyrus reposed in him is shown by the fact that when later Cyrus was summoned to Susa by his father, King Darius, he left Lysander in control of his treasury.

Lysander did not venture to engage the Athenian fleet, and his one victory at Notium was rather invited by the folly of the Athenian commander. But he combated Athenian influence by strongly and unscrupulously supporting the oligarchic parties in various cities and establishing a system of government by boards of ten, δεκάρχιαι. He thus acquired a great reputation and his popularity was such that the automatic end of his command at the end of 407 B.C. was hailed with regret.

He did nothing to help, rather made things very difficult for his successor, Callicratidas, and when Callicratidas died at the Battle of Arginusae, there were demands for his return. Legally the office of ναύαρχος could be held for one year only, but the Spartan government got out of the difficulty by appointing him ἐπιστολεύς, second-in-command, on the understanding that he would in fact be supreme commander, and so he remained till the end of the war.

He continued to interfere in the internal affairs of the Greek cities in Asia Minor and the Aegean, and to establish his system of decarchies. He won credit at home for sending back large sums of money and the numerous personal gifts he received, but the Spartan government was not too pleased with the position he had made for himself. Still he was kept in command, and by his skill and cunning outwitted and defeated the Athenians at Aegospotami. He then sailed for Athens, joined forces with King Agis, and after a siege received the surrender of Athens. Characteristically he was influential in setting up the oligarchic government known as the Thirty Tyrants.

It is recorded that he endeavoured to bring about a revolutionary change at Sparta. This was to substitute for the dual hereditary kingship an elective monarchy. He pushed this proposal by all means at his command, including an appeal to the oracles. It may be that he was hoping to fill this position himself, but he was unsuccessful in his schemes. His countrymen found him too arrogant and overbearing.

In 398 B.C. King Agis died, and the succession was disputed. Lysander supported the claims of Agesilaus and secured his accession. But when Lysander went with Agesilaus to prosecute the war with Persia, he found he had not the influence he expected to wield. In 395 B.C. Sparta went to war with Thebes, and in this campaign Lysander was surprised and killed at Haliartus.

A distinguished and able man, in spite of the moderation of his private life, he yet estranged not only many throughout Greece but also his own countrymen by his unscrupulous political dealings, his arrogance, and his cruelty.

Callicratidas

We know nothing of Callicratidas beyond what is recorded of him during his short-lived period of command, but in these six or seven months words and actions were sufficient to reveal the whole man. Early in 406 B.C. he was sent out to succeed Lysander as admiral of the Peloponnesian fleet, and his was a very difficult assignment.

The Athenians under Conon were for the moment superior. There was great discontent that Lysander was not allowed to continue in command, and Lysander's friends were openly critical. To Lysander's boasts of his success Callicratidas replied in a direct and pointed sentence, and to his critics in the brief, manly, and dignified speech recorded by Xenophon. Lysander had embarrassed him by returning to Cyrus the balance of money in his possession, so that Callicratidas was compelled to go and beg for funds from a Cyrus who rebuffed him. Disgusted by his treatment, Callicratidas declared his contempt for a policy which forced Greeks to fawn on Persians for money, and his ambition to reconcile Athens and Sparta that together they might put the Persians in their place.

Having obtained the funds he needed to pay his men from the Greeks of Miletus, Callicratidas collected a fleet which was now superior in numbers to the Athenian. He sailed to Lesbos and captured Methymna, but to the annoyance of his allies and his own great credit refused to sell into slavery the Greeks taken in this success. He then surprised and blockaded Conon at Mitylene, and leaving sufficient ships for this purpose sailed to meet the fleet which Athens had by desperate measures now collected at the islands of Arginusae.

The weather seems to have been bad in this August of 406 B.C. Callicratidas planned to surprise the Athenians by a night attack, but a heavy thunderstorm prevented this enterprise. Next day he was advised not to offer battle; his fleet was now inferior in numbers to the scratch reinforcements hurriedly sent out from Athens, the more so as fifty of his ships were watching Conon. Declaring that retreat was cowardly, he joined battle. His ships were fighting well when the end came. The trireme from which he was directing the battle rammed its opponent. Callicratidas was thrown overboard by the shock and was drowned.

So died a very fine man. His qualities were shown in his loyalty to his government, his resolve to carry out his orders however difficult and unpleasant the situation, and in his wide Hellenic outlook which could rise above the quarrels of the moment and look to a united and powerful Greece. 'To his lofty character and patriotism,' says Grote, 'even in so short a career, we vainly seek a parallel.'

Cyrus

Cyrus, often called the Younger, to distinguish him from the Cyrus, the Great, who founded the Persian Empire in the sixth century B.C., was fated in the beginning of his career to help Greeks to destroy each

other and at the end to rely on Greeks and by their aid
almost to succeed in his ambition.

The younger son of Darius II and his queen Parysatis,
he was his mother's favourite. Possibly she was
influential in securing for him the command to which
he was appointed early in 407 B.C. The Persian satraps
of Lydia and Phrygia, Tissaphernes and Pharnabazus,
had in the main assisted Sparta, but had not been
satisfied with the result, and the intrigues of Alcibiades
had decided Pharnabazus at any rate to turn to Athens.
Darius determined to settle the matter; the Persian
court had not forgotten Marathon and Salamis, and
Cyrus was sent to Asia Minor to take charge, with 500
talents as a fighting fund. He was still very young, but
showed promise of great qualities which he was destined
never to use to the full.

Cyrus had great personal charm and a strong will.
He was energetic and active in body, not given in any
way to sensual pleasures. Xenophon records in his
Oeconomicus an interesting incident. Cyrus had a park
at his headquarters in Sardis and was showing it to
Lysander. Lysander praised not only the beauty of
the shrubs and trees but also the general scheme and
lay-out. He was astonished to find that Cyrus had
both planned the park and even done much of the
planting with his own hands. Xenophon also tells us
that he was a good judge of character and chose his
friends well. He was munificent in the oriental manner
and went to great trouble to give an appropriate gift to
each recipient of his bounty.

Cyrus was strongly anti-Athenian, and fortunately
for himself found a colleague with whom he could work

and whom he could trust. This was Lysander, who had
taken command just before the arrival of Cyrus. He
was acceptable to Cyrus not only by his gifts as a
courtier and diplomat and a capable man of action, but
also by his personal incorruptibility. It was a new
experience for Cyrus to deal with a man who refused to
accept anything for himself.

Cyrus was thus naturally disgruntled when Lysander
was superseded, and did nothing to help his successor.
After the death of Callicratidas at Arginusae, he was
instrumental in securing for Lysander the extraordinary
command which he held till the end of the war. In
405 B.C. Cyrus was summoned to Susa to his father's
death-bed, and showed his confidence in Lysander by
leaving him in control of his treasury during his absence.

When Darius died, he was succeeded by his elder son
Artaxerxes, one of whose first acts was to arrest Cyrus.
Tissaphernes, the former satrap of Lydia, had viewed
Cyrus' command with jealousy and slandered him to his
brother as plotting to revolt and depose him. Parysatis
secured her favourite son's release, but on his return to
Sardis Cyrus set to work to build up his position. If he
had not previously had the ambition, he was now
determined to dethrone his brother.

In the spring of 401 B.C. he was ready to move, and he
set off with a force which included ten thousand Greek
mercenaries on his march to Susa. The story of the
expedition and its sequel is to be read in the *Anabasis* of
Xenophon, who accompanied it. At the Battle of
Cunaxa, in the summer of 401 B.C., Cyrus very nearly
succeeded. But a lack of coordination in his forces, and
his own impetuosity, led to his death in action. It is

interesting to speculate on what might have happened.
A strong, vigorous, ruler such as Cyrus would have
been, not only would have infused new life into the
Persian Empire, but also might have led another
expedition against Greece, and Athens in particular.
Greece might have become a satrapy of Persia. As it
was, the anabasis of the Greeks paved the way for the
invasions of Alexander.

SECTION 4. GREEK WARSHIPS AND NAVAL WARFARE

The earliest Greek warship was the penteconter
(πεντηκόντερος), a long narrow vessel propelled by
twenty-five oars on each side. At prow and stern there
were small decks. Amidships a single mast supported a
yard and an oblong sail, which was used for cruising but
furled during action. Representations on vases and
reliefs show fighting men and sailors on the decks, so
that the total complement would be sixty to seventy men.

But in the seventh century B.C. the trireme (τριήρης)
appeared. According to Thucydides it was first built at
Corinth. By the end of the sixth century B.C. it had
superseded the penteconter and remained the standard
warship till Hellenistic times.

Unfortunately no trireme has been preserved, and
there are no ancient descriptions sufficiently clear to
settle certain details, but the main outlines are clear.
The trireme was a light, slim vessel, about 120 feet long
and 20 feet wide. It was built of fir, larch, or pine, with
an oak keel. A hard keel was necessary, as warships
were regularly hauled ashore at night. There was a
lofty hooked post at the prow, and a formidable ram of

THE MAIN HARBOUR OF THE PIRAEUS

wood sheathed in bronze below the waterline. Another lofty post was fitted at the stern. On either side of the prow were large holes, resembling eyes, no doubt used for hawsers, as on modern ships. The name of the ship was painted on the prow, or there was some symbol indicative of its name.

Fore and aft the trireme was decked, and on these decks the marines (ἐπίβαται) would take their stand, as would the sailors, whose business it was to attend to the navigation and the general management of the vessel. Awnings of linen or hair (παραρρύματα) were drawn over the centre parts of the ship, at any rate during action. Amidships was a mast, with a yard and oblong sail. The sail was made of linen, the ropes of flax or papyrus fibre. These sails were called μεγάλα ἱστία. In earlier days smaller foresails were also carried. The large sails were used for cruising, but were normally left on shore when a battle was imminent. It will be noted that after the surprise at Aegospotami, Conon, the only Athenian commander to have his ships ready, daringly sailed across the Hellespont and captured the sails which the Peloponnesians had left behind on land. It was therefore impossible for them to pursue Conon's ships.

The trireme was propelled by 170 oars, each rowed by one man. The exact arrangement is a matter of great dispute; experiments have been made using the technique of medieval galleys, so far as that is known, but agreement has not been reached. It seems likely that three men sat on one bench set at an angle to the ship's side, and not in tiers. The rowers were divided into three sections, called θαλαμῖται, ζευγῖται, θρανῖται. The oars were pivoted in leather thongs fastened to wooden thole pins. They must have been twelve or more feet long, and probably thirty spares were carried. Time was set by the κελευστής, who must have been a trained and competent officer. At Athens the poorest class of the citizens, θῆτες, did their national service as oarsmen, and slaves and even resident aliens (μέτοικοι) could be used to make up the numbers required. In the Athenian navy they were paid a drachma a day, more than in other navies, and Lysander endeavoured to tempt them to desert by raising the pay of his own men with money obtained from Cyrus. The trireme was commanded by the trierarch (τριήραρχος). At Athens this office was one of the liturgies (λητούργιαι), duties performed by the more wealthy citizens whereby they made their contribution to the expense of state administration. The state provided the ship and its equipment, and paid the crew. But for a year the trierarch was responsible for its repair and maintenance, and took command. After 411 B.C., two trierarchs were chosen for each ship for the year. With the marines, sailors, and rowers, the total crew of a trireme was about 200.

Anchors were slung from catheads, large timbers projecting on either side of the prow, which also served as guards for the leading oars. For steering two large oars served as rudders at the stern. Ladders were carried, to allow the crew to climb up or down when the vessel was beached, and a number of long poles, presumably for pushing off or clearing other ships.

Normally a fleet was beached at night, as few harbours could contain many triremes. The crew would disembark and get ready their own meal and bivouac. There were no sleeping quarters or provision for eating on board. If, however, a fleet had a longish voyage to make out of reach of land, or speed was essential, some provisions would be taken. Thus a Corinthian fleet sailing for Corcyra in 433 B.C. carried rations for three days. The oarsmen would sleep where they could in rotation or watches. It has been calculated that a cruising speed of at least seven knots was possible, and long distances could be covered in a day, with the help of favouring winds. Thus the news of Aegospotami was taken to Sparta in three days. This means at least 330 nautical miles apart from the mileage overland.

Several points of interest suggest themselves. In the first place there must have been a standard design of trireme, and a constant supply of competent shipwrights. The speed with which losses were replaced makes it clear that it was not a formidable job to build triremes, and they were turned out almost by mass-production.

Secondly, immense quantities of suitable timber were required. It is probably impossible to estimate the weight of a trireme or the amount of timber needed, but as they were turned out almost in hundreds it needs little imagination to realize that there must have been plenty of forests from which the necessary timber could be obtained. Mount Ida in Phrygia was famous for its pines, but the mainland and islands of Greece must have contained vast areas of forest. The demands of the Peloponnesian War alone must have caused considerable deforestation. How many pine trees were needed for the oars of a fleet? A trireme normally carried 170 oars in use and 30 spares. Now at Aegospotami there were 380 ships in the two sides together. If each vessel had its full complement of oars, this means 380 times 200, or a total of 76,000 oars! What acreage of pines would be needed to supply the necessary trees?

Again, the lot of the rowers must have been a hard one. A soldier could see at least something of the battle in which he was engaged. The rower, seated in a confined space, with a high bulwark and an awning overhead, could probably see nothing but the backs of the men in front of him. He had no idea of what was happening, but must ply his oar monotonously, in stifling heat. If he relaxed he would be struck violently by the man in front or behind him, not to speak of that hard taskmaster the κελευστής, who would see to it that every man pulled his weight. If his ship were rammed or sunk by its opponents, the splintered timbers might kill or maim him, or he might not be able to free himself and float or swim till by chance he might be rescued. After Arginusae, one man deposed that he had been saved only by clinging to a barrel until he was picked up.

The Greeks recognized two methods of conducting naval warfare. In the first the fighting was left to the marines on board, hoplites, javelin-throwers, or archers, who used their own weapons to overcome their opponents. The Greeks did not mount catapults or other engines on board, as the Romans and Carthaginians did later. The ships would be locked together and the capture made by boarding. Thucydides gives a graphic account of the battle at Sybota in 433 B.C. between the navies of Corinth and Corcyra. He describes it as exactly like a land battle. So also in the great battle in the harbour of Syracuse in 413 B.C. there was no room for manoeuvring and the conditions of a land battle prevailed.

The second method was developed by the Athenians in the fifth century B.C. In this the ship itself was used as a weapon, and by skilful manoeuvring charged to disable or sink its opponent by means of the ram. Two special forms of tactics were used. In the diecplus, διέκπλους, the trireme broke the enemies' line, passed through, and turning swiftly charged and rammed from

behind. In the periplus, περίπλους, they outflanked and
charged the enemy broadside. This at least smashed
their oars, if it failed to hole the hull. It was necessary
for the oarsman to be very well trained, as clearly it was
essential to back water at once in order to get clear of
the damaged or sinking victim. A high standard of
judgment was also required in those who had to give the
orders. Early in the Peloponnesian War the Athenians
were very highly trained and no other power could
match them in these manoeuvres. But as the war went
on their skill deteriorated, and in the closing years the
Peloponnesians were their equals, if not their superiors
in handling their ships.

Thucydides has left us graphic descriptions of naval
engagements, but it needs little imagination to picture
a naval battle under these conditions—the swift
movement of many ships, the blue waters churned up
by countless oars, the noise of the vessels themselves
almost drowning the shouts of the men on board and
the orders of the officers, broken or sinking hulls, loose
timbers and shattered oars, perhaps with men clinging
despairingly to them, all under a hot and pitiless sun,
till victory or nightfall caused the fleets to draw off, or,
as at Arginusae, a sudden storm ironically brought
peace to the troubled waters.

THE FALL OF ATHENS

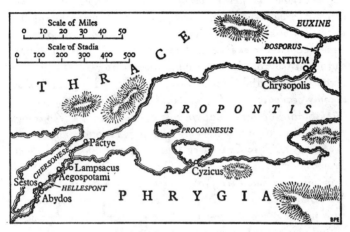

THE PROPONTIS AND HELLESPONT

CHAPTER I. THE BATTLE OF CYZICUS. 410 B.C.

*Cyzicus was a colony of Miletus, founded traditionally in 756 B.C.,
on the southern tip of the island of Arctonnesus, on the
southern shore of the Propontis. The island was joined
artificially to the mainland and so formed an excellent harbour
at which most of the shipping from the Euxine called or took
shelter. As Athens depended so much on this shipping for
corn and other supplies, it was important that Cyzicus should
not be in enemy hands. A wealthy member of the Delian
League, it had recently revolted but had been recovered.
Mindarus clearly realized the importance of the place, and he
would here have the close support of the Persian satrap
Pharnabazus and his army. The success of the Athenians
was largely due to Alcibiades, who showed himself an energetic
and capable commander.*

I

Οἱ δ' ἐν Σηστῷ 'Αθηναῖοι, αἰσθόμενοι Μίνδαρον πλεῖν
ἐπ' αὐτοὺς μέλλοντα ναυσὶν ἑξήκοντα, νυκτὸς ἀπέδρασαν
εἰς Καρδίαν. ἐνταῦθα δὲ καὶ 'Αλκιβιάδης ἧκεν ἐκ τῶν
Κλαζομενῶν σὺν πέντε τριήρεσι καὶ ἐπακτρίδι. πυθόμενος
5 δὲ ὅτι αἱ τῶν Πελοποννησίων νῆες ἐξ 'Αβύδου ἀνηγμέναι εἶεν
εἰς Κύζικον αὐτὸς μὲν πεζῇ ἦλθεν εἰς Σηστόν, τὰς δὲ ναῦς
περιπλεῖν ἐκεῖσε ἐκέλευσεν. ἐπεὶ δ' ἦλθον, ἀνάγεσθαι ἤδη
αὐτοῦ μέλλοντος ὡς ἐπὶ ναυμαχίαν, ἐπεισπλεῖ Θηραμένης
εἴκοσι ναυσὶν ἀπὸ Μακεδονίας, ἅμα δὲ καὶ Θρασύβουλος
10 εἴκοσιν ἑτέραις ἐκ Θάσου, ἀμφότεροι ἠργυρολογηκότες.
'Αλκιβιάδης δὲ εἰπὼν καὶ τούτοις διώκειν αὐτὸν ἐξελομένοις
τὰ μεγάλα ἱστία αὐτὸς ἔπλευσεν εἰς Πάριον· ἀθρόαι δὲ
γενόμεναι αἱ νῆες ἅπασαι ἐν Παρίῳ ἓξ καὶ ὀγδοήκοντα τῆς
ἐπιούσης νυκτὸς ἀνηγάγοντο, καὶ τῇ ἄλλῃ ἡμέρᾳ περὶ
15 ἀρίστου ὥραν ἧκον εἰς Προκόννησον. ἐκεῖ δ' ἐπύθοντο ὅτι
Μίνδαρος ἐν Κυζίκῳ εἴη καὶ Φαρνάβαζος μετὰ τοῦ πεζοῦ.
ταύτην μὲν οὖν τὴν ἡμέραν αὐτοῦ ἔμειναν, τῇ δὲ ὑστεραίᾳ
'Αλκιβιάδης ἐκκλησίαν ποιήσας παρεκελεύετο αὐτοῖς, ὅτι
ἀνάγκη εἴη καὶ ναυμαχεῖν καὶ πεζομαχεῖν καὶ τειχομα-
20 χεῖν· Οὐ γὰρ ἔστιν, ἔφη, χρήματα ἡμῖν, τοῖς δὲ πολεμίοις
ἄφθονα παρὰ βασιλέως. τῇ δὲ προτεραίᾳ, ἐπειδὴ ὡρμίσαντο,
τὰ πλοῖα πάντα καὶ τὰ μικρὰ συνήθροισε παρ' ἑαυτόν, ὅπως
μηδεὶς ἐξαγγείλαι τοῖς πολεμίοις τὸ πλῆθος τῶν νεῶν,
ἐπεκήρυξέ τε, ὃς ἂν ἁλίσκηται εἰς τὸ πέραν διαπλέων, θάνατον
25 τὴν ζημίαν. μετὰ δὲ τὴν ἐκκλησίαν παρασκευασάμενος ὡς
ἐπὶ ναυμαχίαν ἀνηγάγετο ἐπὶ τὴν Κύζικον ὕοντος πολλῷ.
ἐπειδὴ δ' ἐγγὺς τῆς Κυζίκου ἦν, αἰθρίας γενομένης καὶ τοῦ
ἡλίου ἐκλάμψαντος καθορᾷ τὰς τοῦ Μινδάρου ναῦς γυμνα-
ζομένας πόρρω ἀπὸ τοῦ λιμένος καὶ ἀπειλημμένας ὑπ'
30 αὐτοῦ, ἑξήκοντα οὔσας. οἱ δὲ Πελοποννήσιοι ἰδόντες τὰς
τῶν 'Αθηναίων τριήρεις οὔσας πλείους τε πολλῷ ἢ πρότερον
καὶ πρὸς τῷ λιμένι ἔφυγον πρὸς τὴν γῆν· καὶ συνορμίσαντες

ISTANBUL AT NIGHT
looking across towards Scutari, the site
of Chrysopolis

τὰς ναῦς ἐμάχοντο ἐπιπλέουσι τοῖς ἐναντίοις. Ἀλκιβιάδης
δὲ ταῖς εἴκοσι τῶν νεῶν περιπλεύσας ἀπέβη εἰς τὴν
γῆν. ἰδὼν δὲ ὁ Μίνδαρος καὶ αὐτὸς ἀποβὰς ἐν τῇ γῇ μαχό- 35
μενος ἀπέθανεν· οἱ δὲ μετ᾽ αὐτοῦ ὄντες ἔφυγον. τὰς δὲ ναῦς
οἱ Ἀθηναῖοι ᾤχοντο ἄγοντες ἁπάσας εἰς Προκόννησον
πλὴν τῶν Συρακοσίων. ἐκείνας δὲ αὐτοὶ κατέκαυσαν οἱ
Συρακόσιοι. ἐκεῖθεν δὲ τῇ ὑστεραίᾳ ἔπλεον οἱ Ἀθηναῖοι
ἐπὶ Κύζικον. οἱ δὲ Κυζικηνοὶ τῶν Πελοποννησίων καὶ 40
Φαρναβάζου ἐκλιπόντων αὐτὴν ἐδέχοντο τοὺς Ἀθηναίους.
Ἀλκιβιάδης δὲ μείνας αὐτοῦ εἴκοσιν ἡμέρας καὶ χρήματα
πολλὰ λαβὼν παρὰ τῶν Κυζικηνῶν οὐδὲν ἄλλο κακὸν ἐργα-
σάμενος ἐν τῇ πόλει ἀπέπλευσεν εἰς Προκόννησον. ἐκεῖθεν
δ᾽ ἔπλευσεν εἰς Πέρινθον καὶ Σηλυμβρίαν. καὶ Περίνθιοι μὲν 45
εἰσεδέξαντο εἰς τὸ ἄστυ τὸ στρατόπεδον· Σηλυμβριανοὶ δὲ
ἐδέξαντο μὲν οὔ, χρήματα δὲ ἔδοσαν. ἐντεῦθεν δ᾽ ἀφικόμ-

4 THE FALL OF ATHENS

ενοι τῆς Καλχηδονίας εἰς Χρυσόπολιν ἐτείχισαν αὐτήν, καὶ
δεκατευτήριον κατεσκεύασαν ἐν αὐτῇ, καὶ τὴν δεκάτην
50 ἐξέλεγον τῶν ἐκ τοῦ Πόντου πλοίων, καὶ φυλακὴν ἐγκατα-
λιπόντες ναῦς τριάκοντα καὶ στρατηγὼ δύο, Θηραμένην καὶ
Εὔμαχον, τοῦ τε χωρίου ἐπιμελεῖσθαι καὶ τῶν ἐκπλεόντων
πλοίων καὶ εἴ τι ἄλλο δύναιντο βλάπτειν τοὺς πολεμίους.
οἱ δ᾽ ἄλλοι στρατηγοὶ εἰς τὸν Ἑλλήσποντον ᾤχοντο. παρὰ
55 δὲ Ἱπποκράτους τοῦ Μινδάρου ἐπιστολέως εἰς Λακεδαίμονα
γράμματα πεμφθέντα ἑάλωσαν εἰς Ἀθηνας λέγοντα τάδε·
Ἔρρει τὰ καλά. Μίνδαρος ἀπέσσυα. πεινῶντι τὦνδρες.
ἀπορίομες τί χρὴ δρᾶν. Φαρνάβαζος δὲ παντὶ τῷ τῶν
Πελοπηννησίων στρατεύματι καὶ τοῖς συμμάχοις παρακελ-
60 ευσάμενος μὴ ἀθυμεῖν ἕνεκα ξύλων, ὡς ὄντων πολλῶν ἐν τῇ
βασιλέως, ἕως ἂν τὰ σώματα σῶα ᾖ, ἱμάτιόν τ᾽ ἔδωκεν ἑκάστῳ
καὶ ἐφόδιον δυοῖν μηνοῖν, καὶ ὁπλίσας τοὺς ναύτας φύλακας
κατέστησε τῆς ἑαυτοῦ παραθαλαττίας γῆς. καὶ συγκαλέσας
τούς τε ἀπὸ τῶν πόλεων στρατηγοὺς καὶ τριηράρχους
65 ἐκέλευε ναυπηγεῖσθαι τριήρεις ἐν Ἀντάνδρῳ ὅσας ἕκαστοι
ἀπώλεσαν, χρήματά τε διδοὺς καὶ ὕλην ἐκ τῆς Ἴδης
κομίζεσθαι φράζων.

CHAPTER II. AGIS AT DECELEA. 410 B.C.

*After the battle of Cyzicus Sparta offered terms of peace, which
were promptly refused by Athens. In Athens itself the main
result was the restoration of a more democratic form of government, and vigorous operations were taken in the Propontis
under the leadership of Alcibiades. Meanwhile Agis and a
Spartan army still occupied Decelea, only fifteen miles from
Athens, which they had taken and fortified in 413 B.C. on the
advice of Alcibiades who was then in exile at Sparta. While
the enemy were in possession of a fortress in the centre of
Attica, cultivation of the land was impossible, and production*

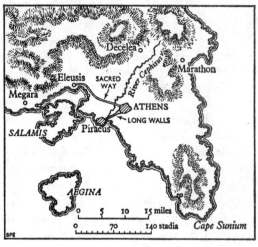

ATTICA

had ceased at the silver mines on Mt Laurium. The overland route also from Delium and Oropus was blocked. But Agis was powerless to prevent the sailing of supply ships into the Piraeus unless the Peloponnesian navy commanded the sea and the trade routes, and that navy had for the time being vanished at Cyzicus. But Athens herself also needed reinforcements, and the energy of Athens in supplying these is to be noted.

Περὶ δὲ τούτους τοὺς χρόνους Θρασύλλου ἐν Ἀθήναις ὄντος Ἄγις ἐκ τῆς Δεκελείας προνομὴν ποιούμενος πρὸς αὐτὰ τὰ τείχη ἦλθε τῶν Ἀθηναίων· Θράσυλλος δὲ ἐξαγαγὼν Ἀθηναίους καὶ τοὺς ἄλλους τοὺς ἐν τῇ πόλει ὄντας ἅπαντας παρέταξε παρὰ τὸ Λύκειον γυμνάσιον ὡς μαχούμενος, ἂν προσίωσιν. ἰδὼν δὲ ταῦτα Ἄγις ἀπήγαγε ταχέως, καί τινες αὐτῶν ὀλίγοι τῶν ἐπὶ πᾶσιν ὑπὸ τῶν ψιλῶν ἀπέθανον. οἱ οὖν Ἀθηναῖοι τῷ Θρασύλλῳ διὰ ταῦτα ἔτι προθυμότεροι

ἦσαν ἐφ᾽ ἃ ᾿ῆκε, καὶ ἐψηφίσαντο ὁπλίτας τε αὐτὸν καταλέ-
10 ξασθαι χιλίους, ἱππέας δὲ ἑκατόν, τριήρεις δὲ πεντήκοντα.
Ἆγις δὲ ἐκ τῆς Δεκελείας ἰδὼν πλοῖα πολλὰ σίτου εἰς
Πειραιᾶ καταθέοντα, οὐδὲν ὄφελος ἔφη εἶναι τοὺς μετ᾽
αὐτοῦ πολὺν ἤδη χρόνον Ἀθηναίους εἴργειν τῆς γῆς, εἰ μή
τις σχήσοι καὶ ὅθεν ὁ κατὰ θάλατταν σῖτος φοιτᾷ· κράτιστόν
15 τε εἶναι καὶ Κλέαρχον τὸν Ῥαμφίου πρόξενον ὄντα Βυζ-
αντίων πέμψαι εἰς Καλχηδόνα τε καὶ Βυζάντιον. δόξαντος
δὲ τούτου, πληρωθεισῶν νεῶν ἔκ τε Μεγάρων καὶ παρὰ τῶν
ἄλλων συμμάχων πεντεκαίδεκα στρατιωτίδων μᾶλλον ἢ
ταχειῶν ᾤχετο. καὶ αὐτοῦ τῶν νεῶν τρεῖς ἀπόλλυνται ἐν
20 τῷ Ἑλλησπόντῳ ὑπὸ τῶν Ἀττικῶν. ἐννέα νεῶν, αἳ ἀεὶ
ἐνταῦθα τὰ πλοῖα διεφύλαττον, αἱ δ᾽ ἄλλαι ἔφυγον εἰς
Σηστόν, ἐκεῖθεν δὲ εἰς Βυζάντιον ἐσώθησαν.

CHAPTER III. THE RETURN OF ALCIBIADES

*The next two years were marked by energetic action on the part of
Athens. Under the vigorous leadership of Alcibiades Thasos
was recovered, and the subjugation of Chalcedon and Byzan-
tium in 408 B.C. gave Athens once more command of the
Bosphorus, which was vital for her corn supplies. The loss of
Nisaea, the port of Megara, and the recovery of Pylos by Sparta
were of less importance to her. The satrap Pharnabazus even
arranged to conduct an Athenian embassy to Susa to make
terms with the King of Persia. Meanwhile the way was clear
for Alcibiades to return to Athens in the early summer of
407 B.C.*

Ἀλκιβιάδης δὲ βουλόμενος μετὰ τῶν στρατιωτῶν ἀποπλεῖν
οἴκαδε ἀνήχθη εὐθὺς ἐπὶ Σάμου· ἐκεῖθεν δὲ λαβὼν τῶν
νεῶν εἴκοσιν ἔπλευσε τῆς Καρίας εἰς τὸν Κεραμικὸν κόλπον.
ἐκεῖθεν δὲ συλλέξας ἑκατὸν τάλαντα ἧκεν εἰς τὴν Σάμον.
5 Θρασύβουλος δὲ σὺν τριάκοντα ναυσὶν ἐπὶ Θρᾴκης ᾤχετο,

ELEUSIS: THE TELESTERION
where the mysteries were celebrated

ἐκεῖ δὲ τά τε ἄλλα χωρία τὰ πρὸς Λακεδαιμονίους μεθεσ-
τηκότα κατεστρέψατο καὶ Θάσον ἔχουσαν κακῶς ὑπό τε
τῶν πολέμων καὶ στάσεων καὶ λιμοῦ. Θράσυλλος δὲ σὺν
τῇ ἄλλῃ στρατιᾷ εἰς Ἀθήνας κατέπλευσε· πρὶν δὲ ἥκειν
αὐτόν, οἱ Ἀθηναῖοι στρατηγοὺς εἵλοντο Ἀλκιβιάδην μὲν 10
φεύγοντα καὶ Θρασύβουλον ἀπόντα, Κόνωνα δὲ τρίτον ἐκ
τῶν οἴκοθεν. Ἀλκιβιάδης δ᾽ ἐκ τῆς Σάμου ἔχων τὰ χρήματα
κατέπλευσεν εἰς Πάρον ναυσὶν εἴκοσιν, ἐκεῖθεν δ᾽ ἀνήχθη
εὐθὺ Γυθείου ἐπὶ κατασκοπὴν τῶν τριήρων, ἃς ἐπυνθάνετο

15 Λακεδαιμονίους αὐτόθι παρασκευάζειν τριάκοντα, καὶ τοῦ
οἴκαδε κατάπλου ὅπως ἡ πόλις πρὸς αὐτὸν ἔχει. ἐπεὶ δ᾽ ἑώρα
ἑαυτῷ εὔνουν οὖσαν καὶ στρατηγὸν αὐτὸν ᾑρημένους καὶ ἰδίᾳ
μεταπεμπομένους τοὺς ἐπιτηδείους, κατέπλευσεν εἰς τὸν
Πειραιᾶ ἡμέρᾳ, ᾗ Πλυντήρια ἦγεν ἡ πόλις, τοῦ ἕδους κατα-
20 κεκαλυμμένου τῆς ᾽Αθηνᾶς, ὅ τινες οἰωνίζοντο ἀνεπιτήδειον
εἶναι καὶ αὐτῷ καὶ τῇ πόλει· ᾽Αθηναίων γὰρ οὐδεὶς ἐν ταύτῃ
τῇ ἡμέρᾳ οὐδενὸς σπουδαίου ἔργου τολμῆσαι ἂν ἅψασθαι.
καταπλέοντος δ᾽ αὐτοῦ ὅ τε ἐκ τοῦ Πειραιῶς καὶ ὁ ἐκ τοῦ
ἄστεος ὄχλος ἠθροίσθη πρὸς τὰς ναῦς, θαυμάζοντες καὶ
25 ἰδεῖν βουλόμενοι τὸν ᾽Αλκιβιάδην.

᾽Αλκιβιάδης δὲ πρὸς τὴν γῆν ὁρμισθεὶς ἀπέβαινε μὲν οὐκ
εὐθέως, φοβούμενος τοὺς ἐχθρούς· ἐπαναστὰς δὲ ἐπὶ τοῦ
καταστρώματος ἐσκόπει τοὺς αὑτοῦ ἐπιτηδείους, εἰ παρείησαν. κατιδὼν δὲ Εὐρυπτόλεμον τὸν Πεισιάνακτος, αὑτοῦ
30 δὲ ἀνεψιόν, καὶ τοὺς ἄλλους οἰκείους καὶ τοὺς φίλους μετ᾽
αὐτῶν, τότε ἀποβὰς ἀναβαίνει εἰς τὴν πόλιν μετὰ τῶν παρεσ-
κευασμένων, εἴ τις ἅπτοιτο, μὴ ἐπιτρέπειν. ἐν δὲ τῇ βουλῇ
καὶ τῇ ἐκκλησίᾳ ἀπολογησάμενος ὡς οὐκ ἠσεβήκει, εἰπὼν
δὲ ὡς ἠδίκηται, λεχθέντων δὲ καὶ ἄλλων τοιούτων καὶ
35 οὐδενὸς ἀντειπόντος διὰ τὸ μὴ ἀνασχέσθαι ἂν τὴν ἐκκλησίαν,
ἀναρρηθεὶς ἁπάντων ἡγεμὼν αὐτοκράτωρ, ὡς οἷός τε ὢν
σῶσαι τὴν προτέραν τῆς πόλεως δύναμιν, πρότερον μὲν τὰ
μυστήρια τῶν ᾽Αθηναίων κατὰ θάλατταν ἀγόντων διὰ τὸν
πόλεμον, κατὰ γῆν ἐποίησεν ἐξαγαγὼν τοὺς στρατιώτας
40 ἅπαντας· μετὰ δὲ ταῦτα κατελέξατο στρατιάν, ὁπλίτας μὲν
πεντακοσίους καὶ χιλίους, ἱππεῖς δὲ πεντήκοντα καὶ ἑκατόν,
ναῦς δ᾽ ἑκατόν. καὶ μετὰ τὸν κατάπλουν τρίτῳ μηνὶ ἀνήχθη
ἐπ᾽ ῎Ανδρον ἀφεστηκυῖαν τῶν ᾽Αθηναίων, καὶ μετ᾽ αὐτοῦ
᾽Αριστοκράτης καὶ ᾽Αδείμαντος ὁ Λευκολοφίδου συνεπ-
45 έμφθησαν ᾑρημένοι κατὰ γῆν στρατηγοί. ᾽Αλκιβιάδης δὲ
ἀπεβίβασε τὸ στράτευμα τῆς ᾽Ανδρίας χώρας εἰς Γαύριον·

ἐκβοηθήσαντας δὲ τοὺς Ἀνδρίους ἐτρέψαντο καὶ κατέκλεισαν
εἰς τὴν πόλιν καί τινας ἀπέκτειναν οὐ πολλούς, καὶ τοὺς
Λάκωνας, οἳ αὐτόθι ἦσαν. Ἀλκιβιάδης δὲ τρόπαιόν τε
ἔστησε καὶ μείνας αὐτοῦ ὀλίγας ἡμέρας ἔπλευσεν εἰς Σάμον, 50
κἀκεῖθεν ὁρμώμενος ἐπολέμει.

CHAPTER IV. LYSANDER AND CYRUS

*Meanwhile, at the end of 408 or early in 407 B.C., Lysander had
been appointed admiral of the Peloponnesian fleet, and soon
after Cyrus arrived at Sardis. Lysander lost no time in
winning the confidence of his seamen and establishing good
relations with Cyrus. For a fuller account of these two remarkable men, see the Introduction, Section 3.*

Οἱ δὲ Λακεδαιμόνιοι πρότερον τούτων οὐ πολλῷ χρόνῳ
Κρατησιππίδα τῆς ναυαρχίας παρεληλυθυίας Λύσανδρον ἐξέ-
πεμψαν ναύαρχον. ὁ δὲ ἀφικόμενος εἰς Ῥόδον καὶ ναῦς ἐκεῖθεν
λαβὼν εἰς Κῶ καὶ Μίλητον ἔπλευσεν, ἐκεῖθεν δ' εἰς Ἔφεσον,
καὶ ἐκεῖ ἔμεινε ναῦς ἔχων ἑβδομήκοντα, μέχρι οὗ Κῦρος εἰς 5
Σάρδεις ἀφίκετο. ἐπεὶ δ' ἦκεν, ἀνέβη πρὸς αὐτὸν σὺν τοῖς ἐκ
Λακεδαίμονος πρέσβεσιν. ἐνταῦθα δὴ κατά τε τοῦ Τισσα-
φέρνους ἔλεγον ἃ πεποιηκὼς εἴη, αὐτοῦ τε Κύρου ἐδέοντο ὡς
προθυμοτάτου πρὸς τὸν πόλεμον γενέσθαι. Κῦρος δὲ τόν τε
πατέρα ἔφη ταῦτα ἐπεσταλκέναι καὶ αὐτὸς οὐκ ἄλλ' ἐγνωκέ- 10
ναι, ἀλλὰ πάντα ποιήσειν· ἔχων δὲ ἥκειν τάλαντα πεντα-
κόσια· ἐὰν δὲ ταῦτα ἐκλίπῃ, τοῖς ἰδίοις χρήσεσθαι ἔφη, ἃ ὁ
πατὴρ αὐτῷ ἔδωκεν· ἐὰν δὲ καὶ ταῦτα, καὶ τὸν θρόνον κατακόψειν, ἐφ' οὗ ἐκάθητο, ὄντα ἀργυροῦν καὶ χρυσοῦν. οἱ δὲ
ταῦτ' ἐπῄνουν καὶ ἐκέλευον αὐτὸν τάξαι τῷ ναύτῃ δραχμὴν 15
Ἀττικήν, διδάσκοντες ὅτι ἂν οὗτος ὁ μισθὸς γένηται, οἱ
τῶν Ἀθηναίων ναῦται ἀπολείψουσι τὰς ναῦς καὶ μείω
χρήματα ἀναλώσει. ὁ δὲ καλῶς μὲν ἔφη αὐτοὺς λέγειν, οὐ

δυνατὸν δ' εἶναι παρ' ἃ βασιλεὺς ἐπέστειλεν αὐτῷ ἄλλα
20 ποιεῖν. εἶναι δὲ καὶ τὰς συνθήκας οὕτως ἐχούσας, τριάκοντα μνᾶς ἑκάστῃ νηὶ τοῦ μηνὸς διδόναι, ὁπόσας ἂν βούλωνται
τρέφειν Λακεδαιμόνιοι. ὁ δὲ Λύσανδρος τότε μὲν ἐσιώπησε·
μετὰ δὲ τὸ δεῖπνον, ἐπεὶ αὐτῷ προπιὼν ὁ Κῦρος ἤρετο, τί
ἂν μάλιστα χαρίζοιτο ποιῶν, εἶπεν ὅτι Εἰ πρὸς τὸν μισθὸν
25 ἑκάστῳ ναύτῃ ὀβολὸν προσθείης. ἐκ δὲ τούτου τέτταρες
ὀβολοὶ ἦν ὁ μισθός, πρότερον δὲ τριώβολον. καὶ τόν τε
προσοφειλόμενον ἀπέδωκε καὶ ἔτι μηνὸς προέδωκεν, ὥστε
τὸ στράτευμα πολὺ προθυμότερον εἶναι.

CHAPTER V. THE DISGRACE OF ALCIBIADES

*After his return to Athens in 407 B.C., Alcibiades seemed to have
re-established himself with his fellow-citizens, and was duly
appointed commander-in-chief of the fleet. In the autumn he
sailed to the scene of operations, and he was expected to continue the task of subduing rebel cities and confirming Athenian
supremacy. But the situation had changed. Cyrus was determined to crush Athens, and through his aid Lysander now
had a powerful and efficient fleet. Alcibiades could do nothing
to provoke Lysander to battle and left his fleet at Notium
watching Lysander at Ephesus to assist his colleague
Thrasybulus, who was conducting operations at Phocaea.
He did a most unwise thing; he left his fleet in charge of a
favourite of his, Antiochus, with disastrous results. Nor
could he manage to control his own excesses. In the face of the
disaster at Notium and bitter criticism of his extravagances,
he once more deserted his city and retired to Thrace, where he
possessed a castle of his own.*

Ἀλκιβιάδης δὲ ἀκούσας Θρασύβουλον ἔξω Ἑλλησπόντου
ἥκοντα τειχίζειν Φώκαιαν διέπλευσε πρὸς αὐτόν, καταλιπὼν
ἐπὶ ταῖς ναυσὶν Ἀντίοχον τὸν αὐτοῦ κυβερνήτην, ἐπιστείλας
μὴ ἐπιπλεῖν ἐπὶ τὰς Λυσάνδρου ναῦς. ὁ δὲ Ἀντίοχος τῇ τε

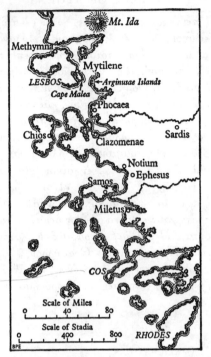

THE EASTERN AEGEAN

αὐτοῦ νηὶ καὶ ἄλλῃ ἐκ Νοτίου εἰς τὸν λιμένα τῶν Ἐφεσίων 5
εἰσπλεύσας παρ' αὐτὰς τὰς πρῴρας τῶν Λυσάνδρου νεῶν
παρέπλει. ὁ δὲ Λύσανδρος τὸ μὲν πρῶτον ὀλίγας τῶν νεῶν
καθελκύσας ἐδίωκεν αὐτόν, ἐπεὶ δὲ οἱ Ἀθηναῖοι τῷ Ἀντι-
όχῳ ἐβοήθουν πλείοσι ναυσί, τότε δὴ καὶ πάσας συντάξας
ἐπέπλει. μετὰ δὲ ταῦτα καὶ οἱ Ἀθηναῖοι ἐκ τοῦ Νοτίου 10
καθελκύσαντες τὰς λοιπὰς τριήρεις ἀνήχθησαν, ὡς ἕκαστος
ἤνοιξεν. ἐκ τούτου δ' ἐναυμάχησαν οἱ μὲν ἐν τάξει, οἱ δὲ
Ἀθηναῖοι διεσπαρμέναις ταῖς ναυσί, μέχρι οὗ ἔφυγον

ἀπολέσαντες πεντεκαίδεκα τριήρεις. τῶν δὲ ἀνδρῶν οἱ μὲν
15 πλεῖστοι ἐξέφυγον, οἱ δ' ἐζωγρήθησαν. Λύσανδρος δὲ τάς
τε ναῦς ἀναλαβὼν καὶ τρόπαιον στήσας ἐπὶ τοῦ Νοτίου
διέπλευσεν εἰς Ἔφεσον, οἱ δ' Ἀθηναῖοι εἰς Σάμον. μετὰ δὲ
ταῦτα Ἀλκιβιάδης ἐλθὼν εἰς Σάμον ἀνήχθη ταῖς ναυσὶν
ἁπάσαις ἐπὶ τὸν λιμένα τῶν Ἐφεσίων, καὶ πρὸ τοῦ στόματος
20 παρέταξεν, εἴ τις βούλοιτο ναυμαχεῖν. ἐπειδὴ δὲ Λύσανδρος
οὐκ ἀντανήγαγε διὰ τὸ πολλαῖς ναυσὶν ἐλαττοῦσθαι, ἀπέπλευσεν εἰς Σάμον. Λακεδαιμόνιοι δὲ ὀλίγῳ ὕστερον αἱροῦσι
Δελφίνιον καὶ Ἠιόνα. οἱ δὲ ἐν οἴκῳ Ἀθηναῖοι, ἐπειδὴ
ἠγγέλθη ἡ ναυμαχία, χαλεπῶς εἶχον τῷ Ἀλκιβιάδῃ,
25 οἰόμενοι δι' ἀμέλειάν τε καὶ ἀκράτειαν ἀπολωλεκέναι τὰς
ναῦς, καὶ στρατηγοὺς εἵλοντο ἄλλους δέκα, Κόνωνα, Διομέδοντα, Λέοντα, Περικλέα, Ἐρασινίδην, Ἀριστοκράτην,
Ἀρχέστρατον, Πρωτόμαχον, Θράσυλλον, Ἀριστογένην.
Ἀλκιβιάδης μέν οὖν πονήρως καὶ ἐν τῇ στρατιᾷ φερόμενος,
30 λαβὼν τριήρη μίαν ἀπέπλευσεν εἰς Χερρόνησον εἰς τὰ ἑαυτοῦ
τείχη.

CHAPTER VI. CALLICRATIDAS

*Early in 406 B.C. Lysander's term of office had expired. He was
relieved by Callicratidas, much to his own annoyance and the
dissatisfaction of Cyrus and his supporters in the fleet and the
various Greek cities where he had set up oligarchical governments under his control. See Introduction, Section 3. How
Callicratidas faced this difficult assignment is related in the
following passage.*

Τῷ δ' ἐπιόντι ἔτει, ᾧ ἥ τε σελήνη ἐξέλιπεν ἑσπέρας καὶ ὁ
παλαιὸς τῆς Ἀθηνᾶς νεὼς ἐν Ἀθήναις ἐνεπρήσθη, Πιτύα
μὲν ἐφορεύοντος, ἄρχοντος δὲ Καλλίου Ἀθήνησιν, οἱ Λακεδαιμόνιοι τῷ Λυσάνδρῳ παρεληλυθότος ἤδη τοῦ χρόνου καὶ

ATHENS: THE TEMPLE OF ERECHTHEUS
ON THE ACROPOLIS
It covered part of the site of the Temple
of Athena Polias, burnt down 406 B.C.

τῷ πολέμῳ τεττάρων καὶ εἴκοσιν ἐτῶν ἔπεμψαν ἐπὶ τὰς 5
ναῦς Καλλικρατίδαν. ὅτε δὲ παρεδίδου ὁ Λύσανδρος τὰς
ναῦς, ἔλεγε τῷ Καλλικρατίδᾳ ὅτι θαλαττοκράτωρ τε παρα-
διδοίη καὶ ναυμαχίᾳ νενικηκώς. ὁ δὲ αὐτὸν ἐκέλευσεν ἐξ
Ἐφέσου ἐν ἀριστερᾷ Σάμου παραπλεύσαντα, οὗ ἦσαν αἱ
τῶν Ἀθηναίων νῆες, ἐν Μιλήτῳ παραδοῦναι τὰς ναῦς, καὶ 10

ὁμολογήσειν θαλαττοκρατεῖν. οὐ φαμένου δὲ τοῦ Λυσάνδρου
πολυπραγμονεῖν ἄλλου ἄρχοντος, αὐτὸς ὁ Καλλικρατίδας
πρὸς αἷς παρὰ Λυσάνδρου ἔλαβε ναυσὶ προσεπλήρωσεν ἐκ
Χίου καὶ Ῥόδου καὶ ἄλλοθεν ἀπὸ τῶν συμμάχων πεντήκ-
15 οντα ναῦς. ταύτας δὲ πάσας ἀθροίσας, οὔσας τετταράκοντα
καὶ ἑκατόν, παρεσκευάζετο ὡς ἀπαντησόμενος τοῖς πολεμίοις. καταμαθὼν δὲ ὑπὸ τῶν Λυσάνδρου φίλων καταστα-
σιαζόμενος, οὐ μόνον ἀπροθύμως ὑπηρετούντων, ἀλλὰ καὶ
διαθροούντων ἐν ταῖς πόλεσιν ὅτι Λακεδαιμόνιοι μέγιστα
20 παραπίπτοιεν ἐν τῷ διαλλάττειν τοὺς ναυάρχους, πολλάκις
ἀνεπιτηδείων γιγνομένων καὶ ἄρτι συνιέντων τὰ ναυτικὰ καὶ
ἀνθρώποις ὡς χρηστέον οὐ γιγνωσκόντων, ἀπείρους δὲ
θαλάττης πέμποντες καὶ ἀγνῶτας τοῖς ἐκεῖ, κινδυνεύοιέν τι
παθεῖν διὰ τοῦτο, ἐκ τούτου δὲ ὁ Καλλικρατίδας συγκαλέσας
25 τοὺς Λακεδαιμονίων ἐκεῖ παρόντας ἔλεγεν αὐτοῖς τοιάδε·

Ἐμοὶ μὲν ἀρκεῖ οἴκοι μένειν, καὶ εἴτε Λύσανδρος εἴτε ἄλλος
τις ἐμπειρότερος περὶ τὰ ναυτικὰ βούλεται εἶναι, οὐ κωλύω
τὸ κατ' ἐμέ· ἐγὼ δ' ὑπὸ τῆς πόλεως ἐπὶ τὰς ναῦς πεμφθεὶς
οὐκ ἔχω τί ἄλλο ποιῶ ἢ τὰ κελευόμενα ὡς ἂν δύνωμαι
30 κράτιστα. ὑμεῖς δὲ πρὸς ἃ ἐγώ τε φιλοτιμοῦμαι καὶ ἡ
πόλις ἡμῶν αἰτιάζεται, ἴστε γὰρ αὐτὰ ὥσπερ καὶ ἐγώ, συμ-
βουλεύετε τὰ ἄριστα ὑμῖν δοκοῦντα εἶναι περὶ τοῦ ἐμὲ ἐνθάδε
μένειν ἢ οἴκαδε ἀποπλεῖν ἐροῦντα τὰ καθεστῶτα ἐνθάδε.

Οὐδενὸς δὲ τολμήσαντος ἄλλο τι εἰπεῖν ἢ τοῖς οἴκοι
35 πείθεσθαι ποιεῖν τε ἐφ' ἃ ἥκει, ἐλθὼν παρὰ Κῦρον ᾔτει
μισθὸν τοῖς ναύταις· ὁ δὲ αὐτῷ εἶπε δύο ἡμέρας ἐπισχεῖν.
Καλλικρατίδας δὲ ἀχθεσθεὶς τῇ ἀναβολῇ καὶ ταῖς ἐπὶ τὰς
θύρας φοιτήσεσιν, ὀργισθεὶς καὶ εἰπὼν ἀθλιωτάτους εἶναι
τοὺς Ἕλληνας, ὅτι βαρβάρους κολακεύουσιν ἕνεκα ἀργυρίου,
40 φάσκων τε, ἢν σωθῇ οἴκαδε, κατά γε τὸ αὐτοῦ δυνατὸν
διαλλάξειν Ἀθηναίους καὶ Λακεδαιμονίους, ἀπέπλευσεν εἰς
Μίλητον.

Chapter VII. Conon at Mytilene. Summer, 406 b.c.

On the disgrace of Alcibiades, ten new generals were elected, with Conon in supreme command. He found the fleet in poor order and was compelled to put many ships out of commission. He had thus a fleet of only 70 ships fit for service.

Meanwhile Callicratidas had shifted his base to Miletus and took the sea with 170 ships. He sailed to Lesbos, where he took Methymna. Conon sailed to help Lesbos, but his fleet was no match for the Peloponnesians. He was driven into the harbour of Mytilene with the loss of thirty ships and blockaded there. It was essential that news of his plight should reach Athens without delay.

Κόνων δὲ ὡς ἔφθη ὑπὸ τῶν πολεμίων κατακωλυθείς, ἠναγκάσθη ναυμαχῆσαι πρὸς τῷ λιμένι, καὶ ἀπώλεσε ναῦς τριάκοντα· οἱ δ' ἄνδρες εἰς τὴν γῆν ἀπέφυγον· τὰς δὲ λοιπὰς τῶν νεῶν, τετταράκοντα οὔσας, ὑπὸ τῷ τείχει ἀνείλκυσε. Καλλικρατίδας δὲ ἐν τῷ λιμένι ὁρμισάμενος ἐπολιόρκει 5 ἐνταῦθα, τὸν ἔκπλουν ἔχων. καὶ κατὰ γῆν μεταπεμψάμενος τοὺς Μηθυμναίους πανδημεὶ καὶ ἐκ τῆς Χίου τὸ στράτευμα διεβίβασε· χρήματά τε παρὰ Κύρου αὐτῷ ἦλθεν. ὁ δὲ Κόνων ἐπεὶ ἐπολιορκεῖτο καὶ κατὰ γῆν καὶ κατὰ θάλατταν, καὶ σίτων οὐδαμόθεν ἦν εὐπορῆσαι, οἱ δὲ ἄνθρωποι πολλοὶ ἐν 10 τῇ πόλει ἦσαν καὶ οἱ Ἀθηναῖοι οὐκ ἐβοήθουν διὰ τὸ μὴ πυνθάνεσθαι ταῦτα, καθελκύσας τῶν νεῶν τὰς ἄριστα πλεούσας δύο ἐπλήρωσε πρὸ ἡμέρας, ἐξ ἁπασῶν τῶν νεῶν τοὺς ἀρίστους ἐρέτας ἐκλέξας καὶ τοὺς ἐπιβάτας εἰς κοίλην ναῦν μεταβιβάσας καὶ τὰ παραρρύματα παραβαλών· τὴν 15 μὲν οὖν ἡμέραν οὕτως ἀνεῖχον, εἰς δὲ τὴν ἑσπέραν, ἐπεὶ σκότος εἴη, ἐξεβίβαζεν, ὡς μὴ καταδήλους εἶναι τοῖς πολεμίοις ταῦτα ποιοῦντας· πέμπτῃ δὲ ἡμέρα εἰσθέμενοι σῖτα μέτρια, ἐπειδὴ ἤδη μέσον ἡμέρας ἦν καὶ οἱ ἐφορμοῦντες ὀλιγώρως εἶχον καὶ ἔνιοι ἀνεπαύοντο, ἐξέπλευσαν ἔξω τοῦ 20

MYTILENE: THE OUTER HARBOUR
looking towards the coast of Asia Minor

λιμένος, καὶ ἡ μὲν ἐπὶ Ἑλλησπόντου ὥρμησεν, ἡ δὲ εἰς τὸ
πέλαγος. τῶν δ' ἐφορμούντων ὡς ἕκαστοι ἤνοιγον, τάς τε
ἀγκύρας ἀποκόπτοντες καὶ ἐγειρόμενοι ἐβοήθουν τεταραγμ-
ένοι, τυχόντες ἐν τῇ γῇ ἀριστοποιούμενοι· εἰσβάντες δὲ
25 ἐδίωκον τὴν εἰς τὸ πέλαγος ἀφορμήσασαν, καὶ ἅμα τῷ
ἡλίῳ δύνοντι κατέλαβον, καὶ κρατήσαντες μάχῃ ἀναδησά-
μενοι ἀπῆγον εἰς τὸ στρατόπεδον αὐτοῖς ἀνδράσιν. ἡ δ'
ἐπὶ τοῦ Ἑλλησπόντου φυγοῦσα ναῦς διέφυγε, καὶ ἀφικομένη
εἰς τὰς Ἀθήνας ἐξαγγέλλει τὴν πολιορκίαν.

CHAPTER VIII. THE BATTLE OF ARGINUSAE. AUGUST, 406 B.C.

Athens rose to the occasion with superb resolution. Within thirty
days 110 triremes were sent out. These vessels must have been
lying in the harbours and dockyards, but they needed crews.

*Every man of service age was called on, and slaves were en-
rolled with the promise of freedom. Resident aliens also were
called on with the offer of citizenship, and many of the cavalry
went on board to serve as marines. It is worth noting that
enough capable men must have been available to provide
officers. To defray the cost gold and silver gifts in the temples
were melted down. Whatever the faults of the Athenian
democracy, these extreme measures in a time of crisis merit
praise.*

*These reinforcements were joined at Samos by ten Samian
vessels and another thirty triremes. The fleet, now 150 ships
strong, sailed to take up a position at the islands of Arginusae,
which lie off the coast of Asia Minor facing Cape Malea at the
south-eastern tip of Lesbos. Callicratidas decided that 50
ships were necessary to contain Conon, but to leave them behind
meant that he had only 120 to face the Athenian fleet of 150.
Still his ships were more skilled in performing the various
manoeuvres of naval warfare. To such an extent had Athens
lost her former superiority. So came to be fought the greatest
naval engagement of the war, in which an Athenian victory
was marred by a tragic sequel.*

Ὁ δὲ Καλλικρατίδας ἀκούων τὴν βοήθειαν ἤδη ἐν
Σάμῳ οὖσαν, αὐτοῦ μὲν κατέλιπε πεντήκοντα ναῦς καὶ
ἄρχοντα Ἐτεόνικον, ταῖς δὲ εἴκοσι καὶ ἑκατὸν ἀναχθεὶς
ἐδειπνοποιεῖτο τῆς Λέσβου ἐπὶ Μαλέᾳ ἄκρᾳ ἀντίον τῆς
Μυτιλήνης. τῇ δ' αὐτῇ ἡμέρᾳ ἔτυχον καὶ οἱ Ἀθηναῖοι 5
δειπνοποιούμενοι ἐν ταῖς Ἀργινούσαις· αὗται δ' εἰσὶν ἀντίον
τῆς Λέσβου. τῆς δὲ νυκτὸς ἰδὼν τὰ πυρά, καί τινων αὐτῷ
ἐξαγγειλάντων ὅτι οἱ Ἀθηναῖοι εἶεν, ἀνήγετο περὶ μέσας
νύκτας, ὡς ἐξαπιναίως προσπέσοι· ὕδωρ δ' ἐπιγενόμενον
πολὺ καὶ βρονταὶ διεκώλυσαν τὴν ἀναγωγήν. ἐπεὶ δὲ 10
ἀνέσχεν, ἅμα τῇ ἡμέρᾳ ἔπλει ἐπὶ τὰς Ἀργινούσας. οἱ δ'
Ἀθηναῖοι ἀντανήγοντο εἰς τὸ πέλαγος τῷ εὐωνύμῳ, παρατε-
ταγμένοι ὧδε. Ἀριστοκράτης μὲν τὸ εὐώνυμον ἔχων

ἡγεῖτο πεντεκαίδεκα ναυσί, μετὰ δὲ ταῦτα Διομέδων
15 ἑτέραις πεντεκαίδεκα· ἐπετέτακτο δὲ Ἀριστοκράτει μὲν
Περικλῆς, Διομέδοντι δὲ Ἐρασινίδης· παρὰ δὲ Διομέδοντα
οἱ Σάμιοι δέκα ναυσὶν ἐπὶ μιᾶς τεταγμένοι· ἐστρατήγει δὲ
αὐτῶν Σάμιος ὀνόματι Ἱππεύς· ἐχόμεναι δ' αἱ τῶν ταξιάρχων δέκα καὶ αὐταὶ ἐπὶ μιᾶς· ἐπὶ δὲ ταύταις αἱ τῶν ναυ-
20 άρχων τρεῖς καὶ εἴ τινες ἄλλαι ἦσαν συμμαχίδες. τὸ δὲ
δεξιὸν κέρας Πρωτόμαχος εἶχε πεντεκαίδεκα ναυσί· παρὰ δ'
αὐτὸν Θράσυλλος ἑτέραις πεντεκαίδεκα· ἐπετέτακτο δὲ
Πρωτομάχῳ μὲν Λυσίας, ἔχων τὰς ἴσας ναῦς, Θρασύλλῳ
δὲ Ἀριστογένης. οὕτω δ' ἐτάχθησαν, ἵνα μὴ διέκπλουν
25 διδοῖεν· χεῖρον γὰρ ἔπλεον. αἱ δὲ τῶν Λακεδαιμονίων
ἀντιτεταγμέναι ἦσαν ἅπασαι ἐπὶ μιᾶς ὡς πρὸς διέκπλουν
καὶ περίπλουν παρεσκευασμέναι διὰ τὸ βέλτιον πλεῖν.
εἶχε δὲ τὸ δεξιὸν κέρας Καλλικρατίδας. Ἕρμων δὲ Μεγα-
ρεὺς ὁ τῷ Καλλικρατίδᾳ κυβερνῶν εἶπε πρὸς αὐτόν, ὅτι
30 εἴη καλῶς ἔχον ἀποπλεῦσαι· αἱ γὰρ τριήρεις τῶν Ἀθηναίων
πολλῷ πλέονες ἦσαν. Καλλικρατίδας δὲ εἶπεν ὅτι ἡ Σπάρτη
οὐδὲν μὴ κάκιον οἰκεῖται αὐτοῦ ἀποθανόντος, φεύγειν δὲ
αἰσχρὸν ἔφη εἶναι. μετὰ δὲ ταῦτα ἐναυμάχησαν χρόνον
πολύν, πρῶτον μὲν ἀθρόαι, ἔπειτα δὲ διεσκδασμέναι. ἐπεὶ
35 δὲ Καλλικρατίδας τε ἐμβαλούσης τῆς νεὼς ἀποπεσὼν εἰς
τὴν θάλατταν ἠφανίσθη Πρωτόμαχός τε καὶ οἱ μετ' αὐτοῦ
τῷ δεξιῷ τὸ εὐώνυμον ἐνίκησαν, ἐντεῦθεν φυγὴ τῶν Πελοποννησίων ἐγένετο εἰς Χίον, πλείστων δὲ καὶ εἰς Φώκαιαν·
οἱ δὲ Ἀθηναῖοι πάλιν εἰς τὰς Ἀργινούσας κατέπλευσαν.
40 ἀπώλοντο δὲ τῶν μὲν Ἀθηναίων νῆες πέντε καὶ εἴκοσιν
αὐτοῖς ἀνδράσιν ἐκτὸς ὀλίγων τῶν πρὸς τὴν γῆν προσενεχθέ-
ντων, τῶν δὲ Πελοποννησίων Λακωνικαὶ μὲν ἐννέα, τῶν
πασῶν οὐσῶν δέκα, τῶν δ' ἄλλων συμμάχων πλείους ἢ
ἑξήκοντα. ἔδοξε δὲ τοῖς τῶν Ἀθηναίων στρατηγοῖς ἑπτὰ
45 μὲν καὶ τετταράκοντα ναυσὶ Θηραμένην τε καὶ Θρασύβουλον

τριηράρχους ὄντας καὶ τῶν ταξιάρχων τινὰς πλεῖν ἐπὶ τὰς
καταδεδυκυίας ναῦς καὶ τοὺς ἐπ' αὐτῶν ἀνθρώπους, ταῖς δ'
ἄλλαις ἐπὶ τὰς μετ' Ἐτεονίκου τῇ Μυτιλήνῃ ἐφορμούσας.
ταῦτα δὲ βουλομένους ποιεῖν ἄνεμος καὶ χειμὼν διεκώλυσεν
αὐτοὺς μέγας γενόμενος· τρόπαιον δὲ στήσαντες αὐτοῦ 50
ηὐλίζοντο.

CHAPTER IX. THE TRIAL OF THE GENERALS. OCTOBER, 405 B.C.

*The Athenians had lost twenty-five ships in the battle, of which
thirteen had already sunk. The remainder, although disabled,
were still afloat and their crews could have been rescued. This
was not done, and all perished except the few who managed to
get to land. Hence came about the celebrated and tragic trial
of the generals on a charge of culpable negligence. When the
news reached Athens the eight concerned were deprived of their
commands and ordered to return home. Six of them obeyed.
Clearly something had happened to arouse horror and anger
in their countrymen.*

*We cannot be sufficiently certain of all the facts to apportion
the blame. It was a matter not so much of collecting for burial
the dead still floating in the water as of rescuing the living, and
speed was essential. In their first despatch the generals stated
that a heavy storm had prevented the work of rescue. When
this was denied by Theramenes, who had been present in the
action as a trierarch, they counter-attacked by declaring that
they had in fact ordered Theramenes himself and Thrasybulus,
another trierarch, with forty-seven ships to perform this duty,
and they had failed to do so. This was not mentioned in the
despatch as the generals considered the storm was a valid ex-
cuse. How soon the storm came up we do not know, but it looks
as if there was some delay in ordering the rescue, and it might
have been wiser for one of the generals to take command of the
operation.*

*The people of Athens, as represented in the Ecclesia, were
certainly to blame for their disregard of the ordinary legal*

*rights of defendants and for their hasty verdict. However, the
seeming scandal of the rescue failure and the unfortunate
occurrence of the great family festival of the Apaturia led the
majority into a rushed decision of which they afterwards
repented. It must be remembered, however, that a large proportion of the citizen body was absent serving with the fleet.
What they thought about the matter and whether their votes,
the votes of those who could judge of the actual conditions,
would have saved the generals, we have no means of knowing.
Some at least were present to give evidence on their behalf.*

Οἱ δ' ἐν οἴκῳ τούτους μὲν στρατηγοὺς ἔπαυσαν πλὴν
Κόνωνος· πρὸς δὲ τούτῳ εἵλοντο Ἀδείμαντον καὶ τρίτον
Φιλοκλέα. τῶν δὲ ναυμαχησάντων στρατηγῶν Πρωτόμαχος μὲν καὶ Ἀριστογένης οὐκ ἀπῆλθον εἰς Ἀθήνας, τῶν
5 δὲ ἐξ καταπλευσάντων, Περικλέους καὶ Διομέδοντος καὶ
Λυσίου καὶ Ἀριστοκράτους καὶ Θρασύλλου καὶ Ἐρασινίδου,
Ἀρχέδημος ὁ τοῦ δήμου τότε προεστηκὼς ἐν Ἀθήναις καὶ
τῆς διωβελίας ἐπιμελόμενος Ἐρασινίδῃ ἐπιβολὴν ἐπιβαλὼν
κατηγόρει ἐν δικαστηρίῳ, φάσκων ἐξ Ἑλλησπόντου αὐτὸν
10 ἔχειν χρήματα ὄντα τοῦ δήμου· κατηγόρει δὲ καὶ περὶ τῆς
στρατηγίας. καὶ ἔδοξε τῷ δικαστηρίῳ δῆσαι τὸν Ἐρασινίδην. μετὰ δὲ ταῦτα ἐν τῇ βουλῇ διηγοῦντο οἱ στρατηγοὶ
περί τε τῆς ναυμαχίας καὶ τοῦ μεγέθους τοῦ χειμῶνος.
Τιμοκράτους δ' εἰπόντος, ὅτι καὶ τοὺς ἄλλους χρὴ δεθέντας
15 εἰς τὸν δῆμον παραδοθῆναι, ἡ βουλὴ ἔδησε. μετὰ δὲ ταῦτα
ἐκκλησία ἐγένετο, ἐν ᾗ τῶν στρατηγῶν κατηγόρουν ἄλλοι τε
καὶ Θηραμένης μάλιστα, δικαίους εἶναι λόγον ὑποσχεῖν,
διότι οὐκ ἀνείλοντο τοὺς ναυαγούς. ὅτι μὲν γὰρ οὐδενὸς
ἄλλου καθήπτοντο ἐπιστολὴν ἐπεδείκνυε μαρτύριον, ἣν
20 ἔπεμψαν οἱ στρατηγοὶ εἰς τὴν βουλὴν καὶ εἰς τὸν δῆμον,
ἄλλο οὐδὲν αἰτιώμενοι ἢ τὸν χειμῶνα. μετὰ ταῦτα δὲ οἱ
στρατηγοὶ βραχέως ἕκαστος ἀπελογήσατο, οὐ γὰρ προυτέθη
σφίσι λόγος κατὰ τὸν νόμον, καὶ τὰ πεπραγμένα διηγοῦντο,

ὅτι αὐτοὶ μὲν ἐπὶ τοὺς πολεμίους πλέοιεν, τὴν δὲ ἀναίρεσιν
τῶν ναυαγῶν προστάξαιεν τῶν τριηράρχων ἀνδράσιν ἱκανοῖς 25
καὶ ἐστρατηγηκόσιν ἤδη, Θηραμένει καὶ Θρασυβούλῳ καὶ
ἄλλοις τοιούτοις· καὶ εἴπερ γέ τινας δέοι, περὶ τῆς ἀναιρέσεως
οὐδένα ἄλλον ἔχειν αὐτοὺς αἰτιάσασθαι ἢ τούτους, οἷς
προσετάχθη. καὶ οὐχ, ὅτι γε κατηγοροῦσιν ἡμῶν, ἔφασαν,
ψευσόμεθα φάσκοντες αὐτοὺς αἰτίους εἶναι, ἀλλὰ τὸ μέγεθος 30
τοῦ χειμῶνος εἶναι τὸ κωλῦσαν τὴν ἀναίρεσιν. τούτων δὲ
μάρτυρας παρείχοντο τοὺς κυβερνήτας καὶ ἄλλους τῶν
συμπλεόντων πολλούς. τοιαῦτα λέγοντες ἔπειθον τὸν
δῆμον· ἐβούλοντο δὲ πολλοὶ τῶν ἰδιωτῶν ἐγγυᾶσθαι ἀνι-
στάμενοι· ἔδοξε δὲ ἀναβαλέσθαι εἰς ἑτέραν ἐκκλησίαν· τότε 35
γὰρ ὀψὲ ἦν καὶ τὰς χεῖρας οὐκ ἂν καθεώρων· τὴν δὲ βουλὴν
προβουλεύσασαν εἰσενεγκεῖν ὅτῳ τρόπῳ οἱ ἄνδρες κρίνοιντο.
μετὰ δὲ ταῦτα ἐγίγνετο Ἀπατούρια, ἐν οἷς οἵ τε πατέρες καὶ
οἱ συγγενεῖς σύνεισιν σφίσιν αὐτοῖς. οἱ οὖν περὶ τὸν
Θηραμένην παρεσκεύασαν ἀνθρώπους μέλανα ἱμάτια ἔχοντας 40
καὶ ἐν χρῷ κεκαρμένους πολλοὺς ἐν ταύτῃ τῇ ἑορτῇ, ἵνα
πρὸς τὴν ἐκκλησίαν ἥκοιεν, ὡς δὴ συγγενεῖς ὄντες τῶν
ἀπολωλότων, καὶ Καλλίξενον ἔπεισαν ἐν τῇ βουλῇ κατηγο-
ρεῖν τῶν στρατηγῶν. παρῆλθε δέ τις εἰς τὴν ἐκκλησίαν
φάσκων ἐπὶ τεύχους ἀλφίτων σωθῆναι· ἐπιστέλλειν δ' αὐτῷ 45
τοὺς ἀπολλυμένους, ἐὰν σωθῇ, ἀπαγγεῖλαι τῷ δήμῳ ὅτι οἱ
στρατηγοὶ οὐκ ἀνείλοντο τοὺς ἀρίστους ὑπὲρ τῆς πατρίδος
γενομένους. τὸν δὲ Καλλίξενον προσεκαλέσαντο παράνομα
φάσκοντες συγγεγραφέναι Εὐρυπτόλεμός τε ὁ Πεισιάνακτος
καὶ ἄλλοι τινές. τοῦ δὲ δήμου ἔνιοι ταῦτα ἐπῄνουν, τὸ δὲ 50
πλῆθος ἐβόα δεινὸν εἶναι, εἰ μή τις ἐάσει τὸν δῆμον πράττειν
ὃ ἂν βούληται. καὶ ἐπὶ τούτοις εἰπόντος Λυκίσκου καὶ
τούτους τῇ αὐτῇ ψήφῳ κρίνεσθαι ᾗπερ καὶ τοὺς στρατηγούς,
ἐὰν μὴ ἀφῶσι τὴν κλῆσιν, ἐπεθορύβησε πάλιν ὁ ὄχλος, καὶ
ἠναγκάσθησαν ἀφιέναι τὰς κλήσεις. τῶν δὲ πρυτάνεων 55

τινων οὐ φασκόντων προθήσειν τὴν διαψήφισιν παρὰ τὸν
νόμον, αὖθις Καλλίξενος ἀναβὰς κατηγόρει αὐτῶν τὰ αὐτά.
οἱ δὲ ἐβόων καλεῖν τοὺς οὐ φάσκοντας. οἱ δὲ πρυτάνεις
φοβηθέντες ὡμολόγουν πάντες προθήσειν πλὴν Σωκράτους
60 τοῦ Σωφρονίσκου· οὗτος δ' οὐκ ἔφη ἀλλ' ἢ κατὰ νόμον
πάντα ποιήσειν.

The speech of Euryptolemus follows in defence of the generals.

Ταῦτ' εἰπὼν Εὐρυπτόλεμος ἔγραψε γνώμην κατὰ τὸ
Καννωνοῦ ψήφισμα κρίνεσθαι τοὺς ἄνδρας δίχα ἕκαστον·
ἡ δὲ τῆς βουλῆς ἦν μιᾷ ψήφῳ ἅπαντας κρίνειν. τούτων δὲ
65 διαχειροτονουμένων τὸ μὲν πρῶτον ἔκριναν τὴν Εὐρυπτο-
λέμου· ὑπομοσαμένου δὲ Μενεκλέους καὶ πάλιν διαχειροτο-
νίας γενομένης ἔκριναν τὴν τῆς βουλῆς. καὶ μετὰ ταῦτα
κατεψηφίσαντο τῶν ναυμαχησάντων στρατηγῶν ὀκτὼ
ὄντων· ἀπέθανον δὲ οἱ παρόντες ἕξ. καὶ οὐ πολλῷ χρόνῳ
70 ὕστερον μετέμελε τοῖς Ἀθηναίοις, καὶ ἐψηφίσαντο, οἵτινες
τὸν δῆμον ἐξηπάτησαν, προβολὰς αὐτῶν εἶναι καὶ ἐγγυητὰς
καταστῆσαι, ἕως ἂν κριθῶσιν, εἶναι δὲ καὶ Καλλίξενον
τούτων. προυβλήθησαν δὲ καὶ ἄλλοι τέτταρες καὶ ἐδέθησαν
ὑπὸ τῶν ἐγγυησαμένων. ὕστερον δὲ στάσεώς τινος γενομ-
75 ένης, ἐν ᾗ Κλεοφῶν ἀπέθανεν, ἀπέδρασαν οὗτοι πρὶν
κριθῆναι· Καλλίξενος δὲ κατελθών, ὅτε καὶ οἱ ἐκ Πειραιῶς
εἰς τὸ ἄστυ, μισούμενος ὑπὸ πάντων λιμῷ ἀπέθανεν. ‖

CHAPTER X. THE STRAWBEARERS OF CHIOS.
WINTER, 406–405 B.C.

*After the battle of Arginusae, the Spartan Eteonicus, who was left
in command by the death of Callicratidas, collected the remnants of his fleet and sailed to the island of Chios. He was
not supplied with funds by Cyrus, and his men were compelled to maintain themselves for a time by working on*

*the land. By the winter they were in desperate straits and a
plot was hatched to attack and plunder the town of Chios.
This incident illustrates the constant difficulty of pay and
supplies which beset commanders compelled to keep a force in
being for long periods. We know nothing more of Eteonicus,
but he was clearly not only a capable but also a wise and tactful
commander.*

Οἱ δ' ἐν τῇ Χίῳ μετὰ τοῦ Ἐτεονίκου στρατιῶται ὄντες,
ἕως μὲν θέρος ἦν, ἀπό τε τῆς ὥρας ἐτρέφοντο καὶ ἐργαζό-
μενοι μισθοῦ κατὰ τὴν χώραν· ἐπεὶ δὲ χειμὼν ἐγένετο καὶ
τροφὴν οὐκ εἶχον γυμνοί τε ἦσαν καὶ ἀνυπόδητοι, συνίσταντο
ἀλλήλοις καὶ συνετίθεντο ὡς τῇ Χίῳ ἐπιθησόμενοι· οἷς δὲ 5
ταῦτα ἀρέσκοι κάλαμον φέρειν ἐδόκει, ἵνα ἀλλήλους μάθοιεν
ὁπόσοι εἴησαν. πυθόμενος δὲ τὸ σύνθημα ὁ Ἐτεόνικος
ἀπόρως μὲν εἶχε τί χρῶτο τῷ πράγματι, διὰ τὸ πλῆθος τῶν
καλαμηφόρων· τό τε γὰρ ἐκ τοῦ ἐμφανοῦς ἐπιχειρῆσαι
σφαλερὸν ἐδόκει εἶναι, μὴ εἰς τὰ ὅπλα ὁρμήσωσι καὶ τὴν 10
πόλιν κατασχόντες καὶ πολέμιοι γενόμενοι ἀπολέσωσι
πάντα τὰ πράγματα, ἂν κρατήσωσι, τό τ' αὖ ἀπολλύναι
ἀνθρώπους συμμάχους δεινὸν ἐφαίνετο εἶναι, μή τινα καὶ
εἰς τοὺς ἄλλους Ἕλληνας διαβολὴν σχοῖεν καὶ οἱ στρατιῶται
δύσνοι πρὸς τὰ πράγματα ὦσιν· ἀναλαβὼν δὲ μεθ' ἑαυτοῦ 15
ἄνδρας πεντεκαίδεκα ἐγχειρίδια ἔχοντας ἐπορεύετο κατὰ
τὴν πόλιν, καὶ ἐντυχών τινι ὀφθαλμιῶντι ἀνθρώπῳ ἀπιόντι
ἐξ ἰατρείου, κάλαμον ἔχοντι, ἀπέκτεινε. θορύβου δὲ γενομ-
ένου καὶ ἐρωτώντων τινῶν διὰ τί ἀπέθανεν ὁ ἄνθρωπος
παραγγέλλειν ἐκέλευεν ὁ Ἐτεόνικος, ὅτι τὸν κάλαμον εἶχε. 20
κατὰ δὲ τὴν παραγγελίαν ἐρρίπτουν παντες ὅσοι εἶχον τοὺς
καλάμους, ἀεὶ ὁ ἀκούων δεδιὼς μὴ ὀφθείη ἔχων. μετὰ δὲ
ταῦτα ὁ Ἐτεόνικος συγκαλέσας τοὺς Χίους χρήματα ἐκέ-
λευσε συνενεγκεῖν, ὅπως οἱ ναῦται λάβωσι μισθὸν καὶ μὴ
νεωτερίσωσί τι· οἱ δὲ εἰσήνεγκαν· ἅμα δὲ εἰς τὰς ναῦς 25

ἐσήμηνεν εἰσβαίνειν· προσιὼν δὲ ἐν μέρει παρ' ἑκάστην ναῦν
παρεθάρρυνέ τε καὶ παρῄνει πολλά, ὡς τοῦ γεγενημένου
οὐδὲν εἰδώς, καὶ μισθὸν ἑκάστῳ μηνὸς διέδωκε.

CHAPTER XI. THE BATTLE OF AEGOSPOTAMI.
END OF SUMMER, 405 B.C.

*Little was done in the last winter of the war. The Athenian fleet
still commanded the Aegean and the Hellespont, but in the
spring Lysander was again in command, in fact if not in name.
He re-established good relations with Cyrus, secured funds
from him, and reorganized his fleet. He avoided a battle when
challenged by the Athenians off Ephesus. Then, in the
summer, he moved. He sailed to the Hellespont and captured
Lampsacus. This threat to their corn supplies from the
Euxine the Athenians could not ignore, and they sailed after
him. Rejecting advice tendered by Alcibiades, whose keen eye
saw their danger, the generals took up a position at Aegospotami on the European shore of the Hellespont, far from
supplies and exposed to attack on an open shore. Lysander
cunningly outwitted them, and the end came quickly.*

*We may ask why so experienced and capable commander as
Conon allowed this. He must have been overruled by his
colleagues (he at least was ready for Lysander's coup), and it
was commonly believed in ancient times that treachery had been
at work. The Athenian general Adeimantus was named as
the traitor.*

*So almost in a few minutes the last battle was fought, and
the long war was over.*

Ἐκεῖθεν δ' εὐθὺς ἐπισιτισάμενοι ἔπλευσαν εἰς Αἰγὸς
ποταμοὺς ἀντίον τῆς Λαμψάκου· διέχει δ' ὁ Ἑλλήσποντος
ταύτῃ σταδίους ὡς πεντεκαίδεκα. ἐνταῦθα δὲ ἐδειπνο-
ποιοῦντο. Λύσανδρος δὲ τῇ ἐπιούσῃ νυκτί, ἐπεὶ ὄρθρος
5 ἦν, ἐσήμηνεν εἰς τὰς ναῦς ἀριστοποιησαμένους εἰσβαίνειν,
πάντα δὲ παρασκευασάμενος ὡς εἰς ναυμαχίαν καὶ τὰ

THE HELLESPONT, NEAR SESTOS

παραβλήματα παραβαλὼν προεῖπεν ὡς μηδεὶς κινήσοιτο ἐκ
τῆς τάξεως μηδὲ ἀνάγοιτο. οἱ δὲ Ἀθηναῖοι ἅμα τῷ ἡλίῳ
ἀνίσχοντι ἐπὶ τῷ λιμένι παρετάξαντο ἐν μετώπῳ ὡς εἰς
ναυμαχίαν. ἐπεὶ δὲ οὐκ ἀντανήγαγε Λύσανδρος, καὶ τῆς 10
ἡμέρας ὀψὲ ἦν, ἀπέπλευσαν πάλιν εἰς τοὺς Αἰγὸς ποταμούς.
Λύσανδρος δὲ τὰς ταχίστας τῶν νεῶν ἐκέλευσεν ἕπεσθαι
τοῖς Ἀθηναίοις, ἐπειδὰν δὲ ἐκβῶσι, κατιδόντας ὅ τι ποιοῦσιν
ἀποπλεῖν καὶ αὐτῷ ἐξαγγεῖλαι. καὶ οὐ πρότερον ἐξεβίβασεν
ἐκ τῶν νεῶν πρὶν αὗται ἧκον. ταῦτα δ᾽ ἐποίει τέτταρας 15
ἡμέρας· καὶ οἱ Ἀθηναῖοι ἐπανήγοντο. Ἀλκιβιάδης δὲ
κατιδὼν ἐκ τῶν τειχῶν τοὺς μὲν Ἀθηναίους ἐν αἰγιαλῷ
ὁρμοῦντας καὶ πρὸς οὐδεμιᾷ πόλει, τὰ δ᾽ ἐπιτήδεια ἐκ
Σηστοῦ μετιόντας πεντεκαίδεκα σταδίους ἀπὸ τῶν νεῶν,
τοὺς δὲ πολεμίους ἐν λιμένι καὶ πρὸς πόλει ἔχοντας πάντα, 20
οὐκ ἐν καλῷ ἔφη αὐτοὺς ὁρμεῖν, ἀλλὰ μεθορμίσαι εἰς Σηστὸν

παρῆνει πρός τε λιμένα καὶ πρὸς πόλιν· οὗ ὄντες ναυμαχήσετε, ἔφη, ὅταν βούλησθε.⁊ οἱ δὲ στρατηγοί, μάλιστα δὲ Τυδεὺς καὶ Μένανδρος, ἀπιέναι αὐτὸν ἐκέλευσαν· αὐτοὶ γὰρ 25 νῦν στρατηγεῖν, οὐκ ἐκεῖνον. καὶ ὁ μὲν ᾤχετο. |Λύσανδρος δ᾿, ἐπεὶ ἦν ἡμέρα πέμπτη ἐπιπλέουσι τοῖς Ἀθηναίοις, εἶπε τοῖς παρ᾿ αὐτοῦ ἑπομένοις, ἐπὴν κατίδωσιν αὐτοὺς ἐκβεβηκότας καὶ ἐσκεδασμένους κᾰτὰ τὴν Χερρόνησον, ὅπερ ἐποίουν πολὺ μᾶλλον καθ᾿ ἑκάστην ἡμέραν τά τε σιτία 30 πόρρωθεν ὠνούμενοι καὶ καταφρονοῦντες δὴ τοῦ Λυσάνδρου, ὅτι οὐκ ἀντανῆγεν, ἀποπλέοντας τοὔμπαλιν παρ᾿ αὐτὸν ἆραι ἀσπίδα κατὰ μέσον τὸν πλοῦν. οἱ δὲ ταῦτα ἐποίησαν ὡς ἐκέλευσε. Λύσανδρος δ᾿ εὐθὺς ἐσήμηνε τὴν ταχίστην πλεῖν· συμπαρῄει δὲ καὶ Θώραξ τὸ πεζὸν ἔχων. Κόνων δὲ 35 ἰδὼν τὸν ἐπίπλουν ἐσήμηνεν εἰς τὰς ναῦς βοηθεῖν κατὰ κράτος. διεσκεδασμένων δὲ τῶν ἀνθρώπων ὄντων, αἱ μὲν τῶν νεῶν δίκροτοι ἦσαν, αἱ δὲ μονόκροτοι, αἱ δὲ παντελῶς κεναί· ἡ δὲ Κόνωνος καὶ ἄλλαι περὶ αὐτὸν ἑπτὰ πλήρεις ἀνήχθησαν ἀθρόαι καὶ ἡ Πάραλος, τὰς δ᾿ ἄλλας πάσας Λύσ- 40 ανδρος ἔλαβε πρὸς τῇ γῇ. τοὺς δὲ πλείστους ἄνδρας ἐν τῇ γῇ συνέλεξεν· οἱ δὲ καὶ ἔφυγον εἰς τὰ τειχύδρια. Κόνων δὲ ταῖς ἐννέα ναυσὶ φεύγων, ἐπεὶ ἔγνω τῶν Ἀθηναίων τὰ πράγματα διεφθαρμένα, κατασχὼν ἐπὶ τὴν Ἀβαρνίδα τὴν Λαμψάκου ἄκραν ἔλαβεν αὐτόθεν τὰ μεγάλα τῶν Λυσάνδρου 45 νεῶν ἱστία, καὶ αὐτὸς μὲν ὀκτὼ ναυσὶν ἀπέπλευσε παρ᾿ Εὐαγόραν εἰς Κύπρον, ἡ δὲ Πάραλος εἰς τὰς Ἀθήνας, ἀπαγγέλλουσα τὰ γεγονότα.

CHAPTER XII. THE NEWS AT ATHENS

Conon had immediately after the battle sent the Paralus with the dreadful news to Athens. It was probably the following night when it arrived. The Paralus was one of the two state

ATHENS FROM THE HILL OF THE MUSES
Looking south-west towards the sea. The Piraeus is
on the far right

*triremes, the other being the Salaminia. They were used for
official voyages and were always kept in first-rate condition.
We learn from the Phaedo of Plato that while one of the triremes
was absent on a sacred mission, no executions took place, so
that the death of Socrates was postponed till the Paralus
returned from its errand to Delos.*

Ἐν δὲ ταῖς Ἀθήναις τῆς Παράλου ἀφικομενης νυκτὸς
ἐλέγετο ἡ συμφορά, καὶ οἰμωγὴ ἐκ τοῦ Πειραιῶς διὰ τῶν
μακρῶν τειχῶν εἰς ἄστυ διῆκεν, ὁ ἕτερος τῷ ἑτέρῳ παραγ-

γέλλων· ὥστ' ἐκείνης τῆς νυκτὸς οὐδεὶς ἐκοιμήθη, οὐ
5 μόνον τοὺς ἀπολωλότας πενθοῦντες, ἀλλὰ πολὺ μᾶλλον ἔτι
αὐτοὶ ἑαυτούς, πείσεσθαι νομίζοντες οἷα ἐποίησαν Μηλίους
τε Λακεδαιμονίων ἀποίκους ὄντας, κρατήσαντες πολιορκίᾳ,
καὶ Ἱστιαιέας καὶ Σκιωναίους καὶ Τορωναίους καὶ Αἰγινήτας
καὶ ἄλλους πολλοὺς τῶν Ἑλλήνων. τῇ δ' ὑστεραίᾳ ἐκκλη-
10 σίαν ἐποίησαν, ἐν ᾗ ἔδοξε τούς τε λιμένας ἀποχῶσαι πλὴν
ἑνὸς καὶ τὰ τείχη εὐτρεπίζειν καὶ φυλακὰς ἐφιστάναι καὶ
τἆλλα πάντα ὡς εἰς πολιορκίαν παρασκευάζειν τὴν πόλιν.
καὶ οὗτοι μὲν περὶ ταῦτα ἦσαν.

CHAPTER XIII. THE SURRENDER AND THE PEACE

It remained to bring the city of Athens to accept terms of surrender.
A siege was the first step. Agis moved from Decelea,
Pausanias, his fellow-king, collected an army from all the
Peloponnesian states except Argos, and joined him, and
Lysander sailed to blockade the Piraeus. Lysander took the
step of giving all captured Athenians the choice of death or
returning to Athens. The result was that ships flocked to the
Piraeus bringing, not supplies of food, but hungry mouths to a
starving city.

The Athenian government did what it could, and the people
showed spirit, but the end could not long be delayed. Largely
through the agency of Theramenes peace was made in April,
404 B.C. That the harsher demands of her allies were whittled
down was due to Sparta. She had not the bitter hatred felt, for
example, by Corinth towards a commercial rival. Besides, an
enfeebled Athens might raise other problems in Greece.

We read in Plutarch that while the allies were debating
what terms to impose on Athens, their hearts were touched by
hearing someone singing a chorus of Euripides:

'And the repeated air
Of sad Electra's poet had the power
To save the Athenian walls from ruin bare.'

There seems to us little in the words quoted (Electra, 167 ff.) *to move hard hearts, and Milton was incorrect in his conclusion. The Long Walls had to go, but Athens was left enough, after eighteen months of bitter party strife, to rise again and play her part in Greece for three generations, till Philip and Alexander changed the world.* *

Λύσανδρος δὲ μετὰ ταῦτα ἔπεμψε πρὸς Ἀγίν τε εἰς Δεκέλειαν καὶ εἰς Λακεδαίμονα ὅτι προσπλεῖ σὺν διακοσίαις ναυσί. Λακεδαιμόνιοι δὲ ἐξῆσαν πανδημεὶ καὶ οἱ ἄλλοι Πελοποννήσιοι πλὴν Ἀργείων, παραγγείλαντος τοῦ ἑτέρου Λακεδαιμονίων βασιλέως Παυσανίου. ἐπεὶ δ' ἅπαντες 5 ἠθροίσθησαν, ἀναλαβὼν αὐτοὺς πρὸς τὴν πόλιν ἐστρατοπέδευσεν ἐν τῇ Ἀκαδημείᾳ τῷ καλουμένῳ γυμνασίῳ. Λύσανδρος δὲ ἀφικόμενος εἰς Αἴγιναν ἀπέδωκε τὴν πόλιν Αἰγινήταις, ὅσους ἐδύνατο πλείστους ἀθροίσας αὐτῶν, ὡς δ' αὔτως καὶ Μηλίοις καὶ τοῖς ἄλλοις ὅσοι τῆς αὐτῶν ἐστέ- 10 ροντο. μετὰ δὲ τοῦτο δῃώσας Σαλαμῖνα ὡρμίσατο πρὸς τὸν Πειραιᾶ ναυσὶ πεντήκοντα καὶ ἑκατόν, καὶ τὰ πλοῖα εἶργε τοῦ εἴσπλου.

Οἱ δ' Ἀθηναῖοι πολιορκούμενοι κατὰ γῆν καὶ κατὰ θάλατταν ἠπόρουν τί χρὴ ποιεῖν, οὔτε νεῶν οὔτε συμμάχων 15 αὐτοῖς ὄντων οὔτε σίτου· ἐνόμιζον δ' οὐδεμίαν εἶναι σωτηρίαν τοῦ μὴ παθεῖν ἃ οὐ τιμωρούμενοι ἐποίησαν, ἀλλὰ διὰ τὴν ὕβριν ἠδίκουν ἀνθρώπους μικροπολίτας οὐδ' ἐπὶ μιᾷ αἰτίᾳ ἑτέρᾳ ἢ ὅτι ἐκείνοις συνεμάχουν. διὰ ταῦτα τοὺς ἀτίμους ἐπιτίμους ποιήσαντες ἐκαρτέρουν, καὶ ἀποθνῄσκό- 20 ντων ἐν τῇ πόλει λιμῷ πολλῶν οὐ διελέγοντο περὶ διαλλαγῆς. ἐπεὶ δὲ παντελῶς ἤδη ὁ σῖτος ἐπελελοίπει, ἔπεμψαν πρέσβεις παρ' Ἀγίν, βουλόμενοι σύμμαχοι εἶναι Λακεδαιμονίοις ἔχοντες τὰ τείχη καὶ τὸν Πειραιᾶ, καὶ ἐπὶ τούτοις συνθήκας ποιεῖσθαι. ὁ δὲ αὐτοὺς εἰς Λακεδαίμονα ἐκέλευεν 25 ἰέναι· οὐ γὰρ εἶναι κύριος αὐτός. ἐπεὶ δ' ἀπήγγειλαν οἱ

πρέσβεις ταῦτα τοῖς Ἀθηναίοις, ἔπεμψαν αὐτοὺς εἰς Λακεδαίμονα. οἱ δ᾽ ἐπεὶ ἦσαν ἐν Σελλασίᾳ πλησίον τῆς Λακωνικῆς
καὶ ἐπύθοντο οἱ ἔφοροι αὐτῶν ἃ ἔλεγον, ὄντα οἷάπερ καὶ
30 πρὸς Ἆγιν, αὐτόθεν αὐτοὺς ἐκέλευον ἀπιέναι, καὶ εἴ τι
δέονται εἰρήνης, κάλλιον ἥκειν βουλευσαμένους. οἱ δὲ
πρέσβεις ἐπεὶ ἧκον οἴκαδε καὶ ἀπήγγειλαν ταῦτα εἰς τὴν
πόλιν, ἀθυμία ἐνέπεσε πᾶσιν· ᾤοντο γὰρ ἀνδραποδισθήσ-
εσθαι, καὶ ἕως ἂν πέμπωσιν ἑτέρους πρέσβεις, πολλοὺς τῷ
35 λιμῷ ἀπολεῖσθαι. περὶ δὲ τῶν τειχῶν τῆς καθαιρέσεως
οὐδεὶς ἐβούλετο συμβουλεύειν· Ἀρχέστρατος γὰρ εἰπὼν ἐν
τῇ βουλῇ Λακεδαιμονίοις κράτιστον εἶναι ἐφ᾽ οἷς προυκαλοῦντο εἰρήνην ποιεῖσθαι, ἐδέθη· προυκαλοῦντο δὲ τῶν
μακρῶν τειχῶν ἐπὶ δέκα σταδίους καθελεῖν ἑκατέρου·
40 ἐγένετο δὲ ψήφισμα μὴ ἐξεῖναι περὶ τούτων συμβουλεύειν.
τοιούτων δὲ ὄντων Θηραμένης ἐν ἐκκλησίᾳ εἶπεν ὅτι εἰ
βούλονται αὐτὸν πέμψαι παρὰ Λύσανδρον, εἰδὼς ἥξει Λακεδαιμονίους πότερον ἐξανδραποδίσασθαι τὴν πόλιν βουλόμενοι
ἀντέχουσι περὶ τῶν τειχῶν ἢ πίστεως ἕνεκα. πεμφθεὶς δὲ
45 διέτριβε παρὰ Λυσάνδρῳ τρεῖς μῆνας καὶ πλείω, ἐπιτηρῶν
ὁπότε Ἀθηναῖοι ἔμελλον διὰ τὸ ἐπιλελοιπέναι τὸν σῖτον
ἅπαντα ὅ τι τις λέγοι ὁμολογήσειν. ἐπεὶ δ᾽ ἧκε τετάρτῳ
μηνί, ἀπήγγειλεν ἐν ἐκκλησίᾳ ὅτι αὐτὸν Λύσανδρος τέως
μὲν κατέχοι, εἶτα κελεύοι εἰς Λακεδαίμονα ἰέναι· οὐ γὰρ
50 εἶναι κύριος ὧν ἐρωτῷτο ὑπ᾽ αὐτοῦ, ἀλλὰ τοὺς ἐφόρους.
μετὰ ταῦτα ᾑρέθη πρεσβευτὴς εἰς Λακεδαίμονα αὐτοκράτωρ
δέκατος αὐτός. Λύσανδρος δὲ τοῖς ἐφόροις ἔπεμψεν ἀγγελ-
οῦντα μετ᾽ ἄλλων Λακεδαιμονίων Ἀριστοτέλην, φυγάδα
Ἀθηναῖον ὄντα, ὅτι ἀποκρίναιτο Θηραμένει ἐκείνους κυρίους
55 εἶναι εἰρήνης καὶ πολέμου. Θηραμένης δὲ καὶ οἱ ἄλλοι
πρέσβεις ἐπεὶ ἦσαν ἐν Σελλασίᾳ, ἐρωτώμενοι δὲ ἐπὶ τίνι
λόγῳ ἥκοιεν εἶπον ὅτι αὐτοκράτορες περὶ εἰρήνης, μετὰ
ταῦτα οἱ ἔφοροι καλεῖν ἐκέλευον αὐτούς. ἐπεὶ δ᾽ ἧκον,

ἐκκλησίαν ἐποίησαν, ἐν ᾗ ἀντέλεγον Κορίνθιοι καὶ Θηβαῖοι
μάλιστα, πολλοὶ δὲ καὶ ἄλλοι τῶν Ἑλλήνων, μὴ σπένδεσθαι 60
Ἀθηναίοις, ἀλλ' ἐξαιρεῖν. Λακεδαιμόνιοι δὲ οὐκ ἔφασαν
πόλιν Ἑλληνίδα ἀνδραποδιεῖν μέγα ἀγαθὸν εἰργασμένην ἐν
τοῖς μεγίστοις κινδύνοις γενομένοις τῇ Ἑλλάδι, ἀλλ' ἐποι-
οῦντο εἰρήνην ἐφ' ᾧ τά τε μακρὰ τείχη καὶ τὸν Πειραιᾶ
καθελόντας καὶ τὰς ναῦς πλὴν δώδεκα παραδόντας καὶ 65
τοὺς φυγάδας καθέντας τὸν αὐτὸν ἐχθρὸν καὶ φίλον νομίζο-
ντας Λακεδαιμονίοις ἕπεσθαι καὶ κατὰ γῆν καὶ κατὰ θάλατταν ὅποι ἂν ἡγῶνται. Θηραμένης δὲ καὶ οἱ σὺν αὐτῷ
πρέσβεις ἐπανέφερον ταῦτα εἰς τὰς Ἀθήνας. εἰσιόντας δ'
αὐτοὺς ὄχλος περιεχεῖτο πολύς, φοβούμενοι μὴ ἄπρακτοι 70
ἥκοιεν· οὐ γὰρ ἔτι ἐνεχώρει μέλλειν διὰ τὸ πλῆθος τῶν
ἀπολλυμένων τῷ λιμῷ. τῇ δ' ὑστεραίᾳ ἀπήγγελλον οἱ
πρέσβεις ἐφ' οἷς οἱ Λακεδαιμόνιοι ποιοῖντο τὴν εἰρήνην·
προηγόρει δὲ αὐτῶν Θηραμένης, λέγων ὡς χρὴ πείθεσθαι
Λακεδαιμονίοις καὶ τὰ τείχη περιαιρεῖν. ἀντειπόντων δὲ 75
τινων αὐτῷ, πολὺ δὲ πλειόνων συνεπαινεσάντων, ἔδοξε
δέχεσθαι τὴν εἰρήνην. μετὰ δὲ ταῦτα Λύσανδρός τε κατέ-
πλει εἰς τὸν Πειραιᾶ καὶ οἱ φυγάδες κατῇσαν καὶ τὰ τείχη
κατέσκαπτον ὑπ' αὐλητρίδων πολλῇ προθυμίᾳ, νομίζοντες
ἐκείνην τὴν ἡμέραν τῇ Ἑλλάδι ἄρχειν τῆς ἐλευθερίας. 80

NOTES

CHAPTER I. THE BATTLE OF CYZICUS

Line 2. νυκτός. Genitive of time within which; see note on Chapter I, line 15 below.

ll. 3, 4. ἐκ τῶν Κλάζομενῶν. Alcibiades had been arrested by the Persian satrap Tissaphernes, but had escaped and made his way to Clazomenae.

l. 4. τριήρεσι. See Introduction, Section 4, page xxxiii. The ἐπακτρίς was a light, swift vessel or skiff.

l. 5. ἀνηγμέναι εἶεν. The perfect optative middle (and the passive) is one of the few compound tenses in Greek. It is required here by the strict historic sequence in Oratio Obliqua.

l. 10. ἠργυρολογηκότες. Athens had in 413 B.C. replaced the tribute or contribution levied on her allies by a 5 per cent tax on imports and exports. It was hoped to raise more money in this way, and it is to be noted that Athens herself paid this tax.

l. 11. διώκειν here seems to mean 'follow closely', as αὐτὸν can hardly refer to Mindarus.

ll. 11, 12. ἐξελομένοις τὰ μεγάλα ἱστία. See Introduction, Section 4, page xxxv.

l. 14. τῇ ἄλλῃ ἡμέρᾳ, 'on the next day'. ἄλλος is frequently used in this sense.

l. 15. ἄριστον. The Greeks normally had two main meals, ἄριστον taken in the late morning (like the French déjeuner), and δεῖπνον, in the late afternoon or evening. So περὶ ἀρίστου ὥραν would mean about 11 o'clock. The Greeks were not great eaters, at any rate in historical times. The main foodstuffs were bread, fish, fruit (especially olives and grapes), beans, garlic, nuts. Honey was used in place of sugar and olive oil for cooking in place of butter. Very little meat was eaten, and milk was commonly goat's milk. Wine was regularly diluted with water.

Note that close together here, we have the three standard expressions of time: genitive, time within which, dative, time when, and in the next sentence but one, the accusative, duration of time.

l. 21. παρὰ βασιλέως. When the king of Persia is meant, the article is regularly omitted.

l. 22. τὰ μικρά, 'the small craft'.

l. 23. ἐξαγγεῖλαι, aorist optative active.

l. 24. ὃς ἂν ἁλίσκηται. The antecedent is omitted; 'proclaimed death as the penalty for anyone who was caught'. Subjunctive + ἄν in vivid sequence.

l. 26. ὕοντος. Notice the genitive absolute use of the participle of ὕει, 'it rains'. Most impersonal verbs use the accusative absolute, e.g., ἐξόν, 'it being permitted', but the subject of ὕει was originally and was always thought of as being θεός or Ζεῦς. πολλῷ is more commonly found only with comparatives.

l. 29. ἀπειλημμένας, perfect passive participle of ἀπειλέω, 'keep off'. Not to be confused with ἀπειλέω, 'threaten', quite a different verb.

l. 34. ταῖς εἴκοσι. The article can be used with a numeral, especially of a round number.

l. 38. τῶν Συρακοσίων. A detachment of Syracusans had arrived with twenty-two ships to join the Peloponnesian fleet, in return for Spartan help at Syracuse against the Athenians.

ll. 45, 46. Σηλυμβριανοὶ δὲ ἐδέξαντο μὲν οὔ, χρήματα δὲ ἔδοσαν. An interesting example of the use of μέν ... δέ. Only the word immediately preceding μέν goes with it or its clause; any word before that goes with both the μέν and the δέ clauses. So in this sentence the first δέ connects with the preceding sentence, and Σηλυμβριανοί is the subject of both ἐδέξαντο and ἔδοσαν. This is often a convenient equivalent for a 'while' or 'though' clause, (concessive) in English, or for a phrase beginning with the word 'without'. 'The people of Selymbria gave them money without admitting them to the city.'

l. 47. τῆς Καλχηδονίας. As with time, so with place the genitive is used to give an area 'within which'. 'In the territory of Chalcedon.'

Chrysopolis, later Scutari, now Üsküdar on the eastern shore of the Bosporus.

l. 48. δεκατευτήριον ... τὴν δεκάτην, δεκάτη, i.e. μέρις, a tenth part or tithe, especially of a customs duty of 10 per cent; a δεκατευτήριον is a place or station for collecting this.

l. 49. ἐξέλεγον. Note imperfect tense, 'proceeded to collect'.

ll. 52, 53. ἐπιμελεῖσθαι ... βλάπτειν. The infinitive, as here, is sometimes used to express a purpose.

l. 54. ἐπιστολέως. The ἐπιστολεύς was the official rank of the second-in-command of the Spartan fleet.

l. 55. ἑάλωσαν εἰς, 'captured and taken to ...'. Note the unusual plural verb with a neuter plural subject. There are several examples of this in Xenophon. Normally a plural verb is so used only when stress is laid on the plurality of the subject, but it is rather surprising here, as γράμματα means 'a letter' or 'despatch'.

This famous despatch is written in the Doric dialect spoken particularly by the Spartans. The first phrase has given difficulty. The manuscripts read τὰ καλά, a neuter plural adjective meaning 'the good things', 'our good fortune', 'our success'. With this reading ἔρρει means 'is gone', 'has vanished'. But it has been objected that such a phrase is not at all what a prosaic Spartan would write, and the scholar Bergk suggested κᾶλα, 'timbers', meaning 'ships', and ἔρρει would then mean 'are destroyed'. But perhaps it is wiser to keep the original reading.

l. 56. ἀπεσσύα, the Doric form of ἀπεσσύθη, aorist passive of ἀποσεύω. This is an unusual word, and may be a Spartan expression. Could it be military slang by any chance?

l. 56. πεινῶντι, contracted from πεινάοντι. In Attic Greek it would be πεινῶσι. Note the ending -οντι, which corresponds to the Latin termination -ant, -unt, etc.

l. 56. τὤνδρες for τοὶ ἄνδρες, τοί being an alternative form of οἱ.

l. 57. ἀπορίομες, in Attic Greek, ἀποροῦμεν (from ἀπορέομεν). This termination also is parallel to the Latin -mus.

ll. 59, 60. ἐν τῇ βασιλέως, i.e., χώρᾳ.

l. 64. ναυπηγεῖσθαι τριήρεις. There must have been carpenters and shipbuilders available. The timber from Mt Ida, pine wood, would hardly be seasoned. See Introduction, Section 4, p. xxxvii.

CHAPTER II.   AGIS AT DECELEA

Line 4. τοὺς ἄλλους. These would be resident aliens (μέτοικοι), and perhaps foreigners in Athens at the time.

l. 5. τὸ Λύκειον γυμνάσιον. The Greek gymnasium was a sports ground, provided and managed by the state, and usually outside the city near a stream. It contained at least a running track and a palaestra, a building with facilities for dressing and undressing and washing, and often a wrestling floor. The Lyceum was one of three gymnasia at Athens. It was on the banks of the river Cephisus, and was elaborate and large enough to contain grounds for riding practice and cavalry parades, jumping pits, and facilities for practising throwing the discus and javelin. ἄν is contracted for ἐάν.

l. 5. ὡς μαχούμενος. ὡς with the future participle expressing a purpose.

l. 7. τῶν ἐπὶ πᾶσιν, 'the rear guard', 'tail of the column'. ἐπί here means 'after', 'following upon'.

l. 9. ἐφ' ἅ is really short for ἐπὶ ταῦτα ἐπὶ ἅ, 'as regards the purpose for which he had come'.

l. 11. ἐκ τῆς Δεκελείας ἰδών. Decelea, 15 miles from Athens, commanded an extensive view towards Athens, and in the clear Greek air it would be possible to see ships entering the Piraeus less than 20 miles away.

l. 12. καταθέοντα, 'running into port'. κατά by itself and in compounds is used particularly of ships coming to land, ἀνά being used for movement out to sea, so ἀνάγεσθαι means 'put out to sea.

l. 14. σχήσοι. This is the only use of the future optative, to represent the future indicative of direct speech in O.O. after a verb in a historic tense. So this = σχήσει in O.R. The future indicative in the protasis of a conditional sentence is always emphatic: 'unless someone is going to seize . . .'. This seems a criticism of the Spartan naval authorities.

l. 14. σχήσω like ἔσχον, is commonly used of momentary action, 'get possession of'.

l. 14. καὶ ὅθεν, 'also the place from which'.

l. 15. Κλέαρχον. Xenophon knew him as a capable officer,

for later he too served under Cyrus. He was one of the Greek generals treacherously murdered by the Persian satrap Tissaphernes. See the *Anabasis*, Book II, ch. 6, 1–15.

l. 15. πρόξενον. The πρόξενος was a public friend, a citizen appointed to represent or look after the interests of another city in his own, performing the duties of the modern consul. So Pindar was the πρόξενος of Athens at Thebes.

Chapter III. The Return of Alcibiades

Line 3. τῆς Καριάς. See note on Chapter I, line 47.

l. 4. τάλαντα. See note on Greek money, Chapter IV, line 21 below. 100 talents would provide pay for the crews of 100 triremes for two months.

l. 6. τά τε ἄλλα χωρία. The Greek order is the reverse of the English; we say 'Thasos and the other places . . .'.

l. 7. ἔχουσαν κακῶς ὑπό. ἔχω with an adverb often simply means 'be' and the adverb is equivalent to an adjective. So here it means 'suffering'. ὑπό, 'by reason of'.

l. 8. στάσεων, 'party conflicts'. στάσις from ἴστημι, or rather, in this sense, from ἴσταμαι, means originally 'taking up a position', 'standing', then the position taken up, 'station', and has a special sense in Greek politics, 'taking a stand', of one political party against another, and so 'civil discord', 'party strife'. See the Introduction, Section 3, p. xviii.

l. 14. εὐθὺ Γυθείου. Of the two adverbial forms of the adjective εὐθύς, εὐθύς is used of time, 'straightway', 'immediately', εὐθύ of place, motion, or direction; with the genitive, 'straight for'.

ll. 15, 16. τοῦ οἴκαδε κατάπλου ὅπως. The genitive depends on κατακοπήν, earlier in the sentence. Almost anything can be done with the article in Greek, as in English: 'the homeward voyage', 'his return home'. In English this would be in the ὅπως clause.

l. 19. Πλυντήρια. The word comes from πλύνω 'wash'. At this festival, which was held on the 20th of the month Thargelion, about the end of May, the clothes and ornaments of the goddess Athena were removed from her statue and solemnly washed by priestesses. This day was one of those on which no sittings of the law-courts were held and no public business transacted.

l. 22. τολμῆσαι ἄν, potential optative—'would dare'.

l. 25. This extract ends at τὸν 'Αλκιβιάδην, which is not the end of the sentence in the full text of Xenophon, but it seemed advisable to omit the remainder of a long and involved period.

ll. 28, 29. ἐσκόπει τοὺς αὑτοῦ ἐπιτηδείους, εἰ παρείησαν. Again, we should put 'his friends' in the clause—'looked to see if his friends were present'. Compare the scriptural phrase, 'I know thee, who thou art.'

l. 32. μὴ ἐπιτρέπειν, 'not to allow', i.e. 'to prevent'. μή is the normal negative with the infinitive.

l. 33. ὡς οὐκ ἠσεβήκει. In direct speech this tense would be the perfect indicative. Occasionally in historic sequence the perfect is changed to the pluperfect indicative, and not to the optative, which could only be used in a compound formation with an auxiliary verb and participle. Note that in the next clause the tense and mood of direct speech are kept.

l. 35. διὰ τὸ μὴ ἀνάσχεσθαι ἂν τὴν ἐκκλησίαν. This is the infinitive form of the past potential phrase οὐκ ἀνέσχετο ἂν ἡ ἐκκλησία. 'owing to the fact that the Ecclesia would not have put up with it.' The μή is due to the infinitive.

ll. 37, 38. τὰ μυστήρια, 'secret rites', 'mysteries'. The word is derived from μύω, 'close the eyes'. At Eleusis, some seventeen miles from Athens, was the sanctuary of Demeter in which mysteries were celebrated in her honour. The chief rites were held in the month of Boedromion (end of September-October), and they included a procession from Athens along the Sacred Way. While the Spartans occupied Decelea this could not take place and communication with Eleusis had to be by sea. The Eleusinian mysteries were the most famous of many such secret rites in ancient Greece, and it had been one of the charges against Alcibiades that he had performed travesties of the mysteries in his house in Athens.

l. 42. τρίτῳ μηνί. Some editors emend to τετάρτῳ, as more than three months had elapsed between the Plynteria in May and the end of September.

ll. 49, 50. τροπαῖον ... ἔστησε. As a token of undisputed victory it was the custom after a battle for the victors to erect a monument of wood or stone or of captured arms on the site of the battle.

l. 51. ἐπολέμει. Note the imperfect tense, 'continued the war'.

CHAPTER IV. LYSANDER AND CYRUS

Line 2. Κρατησιππίδᾳ. Dative of the person concerned, equivalent here to a possessive. The office of ναύαρχος at this time was held for one year only.

l. 8. πεποιηκὼς εἴη. Here we have a pluperfect optative; see note on Chapter III, line 33. Optative as being virtual indirect speech: 'the things which he was alleged to have done.'

ll. 8, 9. ὡς προθυμοτάτου ... γενέσθαι. The adjective is assimilated to the case of Κύρου.

l. 13. ἐὰν δὲ καὶ ταῦτα, i.e. ἐκλίπῃ.

ll. 13, 14. κατακόψειν. κατακόπτω is regularly used in this sense of 'cutting up' bullion, 'coining into money'.

l. 15. ἐκέλευον. Notice the imperfect, 'kept bidding', 'urged'.

ll. 15, 16. δραχμὴν, 'Αττικήν. See below for the value of this.

l. 15. τῷ ναύτῃ, 'per sailor'.

l. 18. ἀναλώσει, i.e. ὁ Κῦρος.

One can hardly imagine Athenian citizens deserting, but aliens and even slaves were serving with the fleet.

21. μνᾶς (and ὄβελον below). Each Greek state had its own coinage; relatively the table of values was the same in each.

6 obols	= 1 drachma
100 drachmas	= 1 mina
60 minas	= 1 talent.

The obol, drachma, and mina were silver coins, the talent uncoined bullion measured by weight. There were two main standards or rates of exchange, the Aeginetan and the Attic; ten Aeginetan obols were reckoned as equal to 6 Attic obols. It is almost impossible in these days to give any general modern equivalent. Money is worth what it will do, and its value is relative to the cost of living. Authorities writing before 1914–19, when the great inflation began, give the obol as worth 1½d.; so a drachma was worth 9d. (roughly the Roman denarius), a mina 75s., and a talent about £225. But it has been reckoned that 3 obols a day or 180 drachmas a year would suffice for an Athenian to keep himself and a wife and home for a year. A drachma seems to have been a normal day's wage in Athens at the end of the fifth century B.C. Compare with this the 4d. which was a common day's wage for a journeyman in the reign of Elizabeth I. For a most interesting discussion of the matter see the *Cambridge Ancient History*, Vol. V, Ch. 1. At the time of the Sicilian Expedition Athenian sailors received a drachma per day (*Thuc.* VI, 31, 3), but according to information given to the Spartans by Alcibiades (*Thuc.* VIII, 15, 2) this was later cut to three obols, which the Peloponnesian seamen also received. So the 30 minas (½ talent) per ship would pay the crew of 200 for a month. In the Royal Navy an ordinary seaman received 19s. per month from the time of the Commonwealth to the end of the eighteenth century, which amounts to 7½d. a day. This was in addition to rations, but not clothing, whereas the Greek sailor had to provide his own food. What arrangements, if any, were made for the Greeks to get money to their wives and families we do not know.

l. 27. προσοφειλόμενον. This seems to mean 'owing in addition to what had been paid', i.e. 'arrears'. μηνός: supply μισθόν. So he paid up what was owing and added a month's pay in advance.

CHAPTER V. THE DISGRACE OF ALCIBIADES

Line 2. τειχίζειν, 'was fortifying', perhaps to make it his base of operations, but there seems something wrong about this as Phocaea was not on the side of the Athenians and some Peloponnesian ships took refuge there after their defeat at Arginusae.

l. 3. 'Αντίοχον. According to Plutarch, Antiochus had first won the favour of Alcibiades by catching a tame quail which had escaped. Plutarch describes him as a good helmsman but silly and vulgar. This episode reminds us of Drake at Cadiz, but Drake did not act for pure ostentation and managed things better.

l. 12. ἤνοιξεν is a rare form of the aorist of ἀνοίγνυμι, as if from ἀνοίγω.. So also in Ch. VII, line 22 the rare imperfect ἤνοιγον is used. οἱ μὲν, Lysander's ships.

l. 13. διεσπαρμέναις ταῖς ναυσί. Dative of accompaniment, 'with their ships in disorder'.

l. 21. πολλαῖς ναυσὶν ἐλαττοῦσθαι. This does not seem to be the normal dative with ἐλαττοῦμαι 'inferior in ships', but rather giving the measure of difference, 'many ships inferior'.

l. 23. ἐν οἴκῳ, 'at home'.

l. 25. ἀκρατείαν. It was Alcibiades' great weakness not to be able to control his temperament.

ll. 26–8. This list of generals is important, as they were the generals concerned at the battle of Arginusae. Pericles was the son of the great Athenian leader and statesman. It was not usual for a Greek to bear his father's name. We hear no more of one, Leon, and in his place appears the name Lysias: unless Leon here is a mistake, we do not know the explanation.

l. 29. πονηρῶς . . . φερόμενος, 'having a bad reputation'.

ll. 30, 31. τὰ ἑαυτοῦ τείχη. This castle was at Pactye, in Thrace, on the shores of the Propontis, about twelve miles from the entrance to the Hellespont. We do not know how or when it became the private property of Alcibiades.

CHAPTER VI. CALLICRATIDAS

Line 1. ἡ σελήνη ἐξέλιπεν. This eclipse took place on 15 April, 406 B.C.

ll. 1, 2. ὁ παλαιὸς τῆς Ἀθηνᾶς νεὼς. The temple of Athena Polias, on the north side of the Acropolis; part of the site of this temple was built over when the Erectheum was reconstructed, also after a fire.

ll. 2, 3. Πιτύα . . . ἐφορεύοντος. Pityas would be the senior ephor, who gave his name to the year. Similarly at Athens the senior of the nine archons gave his name to the year and was called ἐπώνυμος. So at Rome the names of the consuls gave the date. It may be added that these datings, as well as the phrase τῷ πολέμῳ . . . ἐτῶν, are thought by some scholars to have been added to the text by a later hand or incorporated from a note written in by some scribe.

l. 4. χρόνου, 'period of office'.

ll. 8–11. ἐκέλευσεν . . . παραδοῦναι, καὶ ὁμολογήσειν. A rather condensed sentence, and we must understand ἔφη from ἐκέλευσεν. 'he (Callicratidas) ordered Lysander to hand over the ships, and said he (Callicratidas) would admit that he (Lysander) had command of the sea . . .'.

ll. 11–12. οὐ φαμένου . . . πολυπραγμονεῖν. οὐ φημί, like nego in Latin, means 'say . . . not'.

l. 12. ἄλλου ἄρχοντος, 'while another was in command'.

l. 13. πρὸς αἷς. Relative attraction for πρὸς ταύταις ἅς. . . .'

l. 22. γιγνομένων, 'being appointed'. γίγνομαι is often thus used in a passive sense.

ll. 23, 24. τι παθεῖν, 'suffer some disaster'.

l. 24. ἐκ τούτου δέ. . . . This use of δέ does not connect a new clause but emphasizes the main clause; as it often occurs in the apodosis of conditional sentences, it is known grammatically as 'δέ in apodosi'.

ll. 26–33. A manly and dignified speech.

l. 27. βούλεται, 'claims'.

l. 28. τὸ κατ' ἐμέ, 'so far as I am concerned'.

ll. 30, 31. πρὸς ἃ ἐγώ τε φιλοτιμοῦμαι καὶ ἡ πόλις αἰτιάζεται. ἅ = ταῦτα ἅ; the accusative is not quite the same with the two verbs; ἅ φιλοτιμοῦμαι 'for which I have ambitions', ἅ αἰτιάζεται 'of which the city is accused'.

l. 33. τὰ καθεστῶτα, 'the situation'.

l. 40. σωθῇ οἴκαδε, 'get safe home'.

l. 41. διαλλάξειν Ἀθηναίους καὶ Λακεδαιμονίους. This attitude was perhaps taken by other Spartans and goes far to explain the comparatively easy terms given to Athens in the peace of 404 B.C. by Sparta to the disgust of some of her more vindictive allies.

CHAPTER. VII. CONON AT MITYLENE. SUMMER, 406 B.C.

Line 8. This success induced Cyrus at last to be more cooperative.

l. 10. σίτων . . . ἦν εὐπορῆσαι. ἦν, 'it was possible to get good supplies'. Genitive as with most verbs signifying fulness and want.

ll. 14, 15. εἰς κοίλην ναῦν, 'into the hold'. The marines would normally have their place on the decks.

l. 17. ὡς ... εἶναι. ὡς = ὥστε in a consecutive clause is not normally found in Attic prose apart from Xenophon.

ll. 21, 22. τὸ πέλαγος, 'the open sea'.

l. 24. ἀριστοποιούμενοι. It was ἤδη μέσον ἡμέρας. See the note on Greek meals in Chapter I, line 15.

CHAPTER VIII. THE BATTLE OF ARGINUSAE.
AUGUST, 406 B.C.

Line 3. ταῖς δὲ εἴκοσι καὶ ἑκατόν. The article is sometimes used, as here, to give a number which is part of a whole, though the whole is not given. 'Callicratidas left fifty . . . and with the hundred and twenty (which were left). . . .'

ll. 8, 9. περὶ μέσας νύκτας. The plural is regularly used in phrases expressing midnight.

l. 11. ἄνεσχεν, 'held up', 'ceased', i.e. the rain.

l. 15. ἐπετέτακτο, 'was drawn up behind'.

l. 18. ἐχόμεναι, 'holding on to', i.e. 'next to'.

ll. 18, 19. ταξιάρχων. The ταξίαρχος at Athens was strictly the commander of a τάξις or quota of infantry raised by each tribe; here it is used in a wider sense of the various naval officers below the rank of general.

l. 19. ἐπὶ μιᾶς, 'in single line', 'one deep'.

ll. 24, 25. διέκπλουν διδοῖεν, 'give them the chance to use the diecplus'. For the meaning of this and periplus below see the Introduction, Section 4.

l. 25. χεῖρον ... ἔπλεον, 'sailed worse', i.e. 'were worse at manoeuvring'.

l. 30. εἴη καλῶς ἔχον. εἰμί is sometimes used, as here, as an auxiliary verb with a participle instead of the finite verb. So εἴη ἔχον = ἔχοι.

l. 32. οὐδὲν μὴ κάκιον οἰκεῖται. οὐδέν is a stronger form of οὐ 'in no respect'. οὐ μή is used with the future indicative (also with the subjunctive, especially with the aorist) to make an emphatic future denial. The manuscripts read οἰκεῖται, which is a present indicative, and this construction is not elsewhere found with this tense. Various emendations have been suggested, but could this possibly be a colloquial usage? Or could a present be justified? 'Sparta is no worse off.' Xenophon is giving the actual words, which must have been related to him, or at least remembered and reported. These words of Callicratidas certainly became famous. Cicero refers to it in the *De Officiis*, I. 24.

l. 35. ἐμβαλούσης τῆς νεώς, i.e. when his ship rammed another, the shock threw him overboard. He would be standing on the decked portion of the trireme.

l. 41. αὐτοῖς ἀνδράσιν, 'men and all'.

l. 43. πασῶν οὐσῶν δέκα, 'being ten in all'.

l. 47. καταδεδυκυίας, 'disabled' or 'waterlogged', not 'sunk'. The point is that these ships were still afloat though helpless, and their crews could have been rescued.

ll. 47, 48. ταῖς δὲ ἄλλαις, supply πλεῖν.

l. 49. ἄνεμος καὶ χειμών. The weather seems to have been generally bad; rain and thunder the previous evening had prevented Callicratidas from delivering his surprise attack on the Athenians.

CHAPTER IX. THE TRIAL OF THE GENERALS.
OCTOBER, 405 B.C.

Line 4. οὐκ ἀπῆλθον, i.e. they went into voluntary exile. We do not know what subsequently happened to them. Of the ten generals Conon was blockaded at Mitylene, and Archestratus had died, so that eight were present at Arginusae.

l. 7. ὁ τοῦ δήμου τότε προεστηκώς, 'the leader of the democratic party at that time'; not an official position. Archedemus was ridiculed by the comic poets and accused of embezzlement and corruption.

l. 8. τῆς διωβελίας, a payment of two obols a day; some form of public assistance for needy citizens, but details of qualifications and payment are not known.

l. 8. ἐπιβολήν, a fine inflicted by a magistrate summarily in virtue of his office. Erasinides was first fined and then formally prosecuted περὶ τῆς στρατηγίας. Was this an anticipation of the charge brought against the whole body of generals?

l. 14. Τιμοκράτους, of Timocrates, like Callixenus and others who took part in this trial, nothing else is known.

l. 17. Θηραμένης. See Introduction, Section 3, p. xxiii.

l. 17. δικαίους εἶναι λόγον ὑποσχεῖν. The Indirect Speech depends on the idea of saying in κατηγόρουν. 'saying that they were bound to render account'.

l. 19. ἐπεδείκνυε is a rare form of the imperfect of ἐπιδείκνυμι.

ll. 20–2. οἱ στρατηγοί ... ἕκαστος ἀπελογήσατο. The singular verb agrees with ἕκαστος, the nearest subject.

l. 23. κατὰ τὸν νόμον. It was not yet a formal trial, in which a set time would be allowed for speeches, measured by the clepsydra or water-clock.

l. 29. οὐχ, ὅτι ... οὐχ goes with ψευσόμεθα: 'we shall not, just because they accuse us, state falsely that they are to blame . . .'.

l. 33. ἔπειθον. Note the imperfect, 'they were convincing'.

l. 36. τὰς χεῖρας οὐκ ἂν καθεώρων. The voting was by show of hands. κατα in καθεώρων means 'clearly'.

l. 37. προβουλεύσασαν εἰσενεγκεῖν. . . . The construction carries on with ἔδοξε after the parenthesis. It was a function of the βουλή to prepare a motion, προβούλευμα, beforehand for submission to the ecclesia.

l. 37. κρίνοιντο. Indirect deliberative question: 'by what procedure the men were to be tried'.

l. 38. 'Απατόυρια. This feast took place in the month of Pyanepsion (October-November); it was celebrated by all the Ionic Greeks, but particularly by the Athenians, by the φρατρίαι or family groups. It lasted for three days, included sacrifices and family gatherings, and was the occasion for the registration or enrolling of children, young men, and newly-married wives in the φρατρία.

ll. 38, 39. οἱ περὶ τὸν Θηραμένην, 'Theramenes and his party'.

l. 41. ἐν χρῷ κεκαρμένους, 'close-shaved', i.e. their heads. This form of the dative is found only in this phrase.

l. 47. τοὺς ἀρίστους . . . γενομένους. The regular Greek expression for 'behave with great gallantry'.

l. 48. παράνομα συγγεγραφέναι, 'had proposed an illegal measure', a feature of Athenian law was the γραφὴ παρανόμων, 'an indictment for an illegal proposal', to which anyone making a proposal in the ecclesia was liable. It was intended as a safeguard against any attempt to subvert the constitution, but it could be used as a political weapon. Compare the wrangles of Aeschines and Demosthenes fifty years later.

l. 52. ἐπὶ τούτοις, 'on the strength of this': τούτους 'Euryptolemus and his friends'.

l. 55. τῶν πρυτάνεων. Each of the ten tribes provided fifty members of the boule or council of five hundred, and each fifty took it in turn to serve for one tenth of the year as a committee to prepare the agenda and deal with matters of urgency; they also elected the chairman of the ecclesia for each meeting.

l. 58. οἱ δὲ ἐβόων, i.e. those present in the ecclesia. ἐβόων is equivalent to a verb of command.

l. 59. πλὴν Σωκράτους. See Introduction, Section 3, p. xxv. Xenophon says in the Memorabilia (I. 1. 18) that Socrates was the ἐπιστάτης or chairman on this occasion. Socrates himself is made to refer to the incident in Plato's Apology, (32. A–C).

l. 60. κατὰ νόμον. The legal position was not quite clear. The psephism or decree of Cannonus (who he was is not known) seems to have been a working principle rather than a definite law. But it was at least understood that defendants must be tried separately and not in a body.

l. 64. ἡ τῆς βουλῆς, i.e. γνώμη.

l. 66. ὑπομοσαμένου, 'having made an objection on oath'. The voting was apparently very close for the result to be challenged.

l. 73. ἐδέθησαν. Those who stood bail for an accused person held him in custody till he was required to appear for trial.

ll. 74–5. στάσεώς . . . ἐν ᾗ Κλεοφῶν ἀπέθανεν. Xenophon does not tell us anything more about this στάσις. Cleophon, a leader of the democratic party, helped in the restoration of the democracy in 410 B.C. Honest but violent in manner, he was a capable financier and introduced the diobelia or payment to needy citizens. He consistently opposed any suggestion of peace with Sparta, and this opposition when the situation was hopeless led to a disturbance in which he was prosecuted on a charge of evading military service and condemned and executed early in 404 B.C.

l. 76. οἱ ἐκ Πειραιῶς. The opponents of the Thirty Tyrants

under Thrasybulus established themselves at Munychia in the Piraeus, whence they successfully cleared Athens of the Thirty and restored the democracy.

CHAPTER X. THE STRAWBEARERS OF CHIOS.
WINTER, 406–405 B.C.

Line 2. ἀπὸ τῆς ὥρας, 'kept themselves on the season', i.e. 'on the fruits of the season, the harvest'.

l. 3. μισθοῦ, genitive of price, 'for hire'.

l. 4. γυμνοί, not necessarily 'naked', but 'lightly clad' or 'inadequately clad'. It often means 'with the undergarment only', and so could mean 'without uniform'.

l. 4. ἀνυπόδητοι. Shoes or sandals would wear out quickly.

l. 5. τῇ Χίῳ, the main town of the island. These small islands often had one town only which bore the same name. No doubt this is the explanation of the old Latin rule about 'towns and small islands'.

l. 6. ἀρέσκοι, indefinite construction. 'any who', 'all who'.

l. 6. κάλαμον. Strictly, κάλαμος is a reed or stalk, καλάμη a corn-stalk or piece of straw. But κάλαμος is also used for a corn-stalk, and Xenophon calls them καλαμήφοροι. It seems pedantic to ask whether the sign was actually a piece of reed or a straw. No doubt any stalk would serve the purpose.

l. 7. σύνθημα, 'badge', 'sign', often used of a password.

l. 8. τί χρῷτο, indirect deliberative question. 'How he was to deal with the matter.'

l. 9. ἐκ τοῦ ἐμφανοῦς, 'openly'.

l. 12. πάντα τὰ πράγματα, 'the situation generally'; 'upset the applecart'.

ll. 14–15. σχοῖεν ... ὦσιν. Note the change from strict to vivid sequence, but there seems no real difference in meaning.

l. 18. ἰατρείου, 'surgery'. The man appears to have gone to a doctor in the town. Did the Greeks have medical officers attached to their forces? If it was the official doctor, the translation would be 'sick bay', the man being a sailor.

l. 18. ἀπέκτεινε, 'had him killed'. An unlucky ending to a visit to the doctor.

l. 22. ἀεὶ ὁ ἀκούων, 'each man as he heard . . .'.

l. 26. ἐσήμηνεν. Although this verb is commonly used of the bugler who gives the signal or is impersonal, the subject here is probably Eteonicus, 'had the signal given'.

CHAPTER XI. THE BATTLE OF AEGOSPOTAMI.
END OF SUMMER, 405 B.C.

Line 1. ἐκεῖθεν, from Sestos.

ll. 1, 2. 'Αιγὸς ποταμούς. Aegospotami, so called from two small streams which fall from the hills of Gallipoli into the Dardanelles, is about half way between Sestos and Lampsacus. By opposite to Lampsacus Xenophon must mean on the European shore, and not directly across the straits. He must have seen the site of the battle during his journeyings.

l. 3. σταδίους ὡς πεντεκαίδεκα; the singular is στάδιον. Both στάδια and στάδιοι are used as the plural form, sometimes even in the same passage, e.g. Thucydides VII. 78. A stade is 600 Greek feet = 606¾ English feet. So a stade is rather less than a furlong and 15, just under 1¾ miles, about 3000 yards.

l. 7. παραβλήματα, the same as παραρρύματα. See Introduction, Section 4, p. xxxiv. Conon also used these awnings for concealment purposes, Chapter 7.

ll. 7–8. προεῖπεν ὡς μηδεὶς κινήσοιτο . . . ἀνάξοιτο.. The future optative is used only in indirect speech to represent the future indicative of direct speech. See note on Chapter II, line 14. Here the future in direct speech would be used as a command; 'no one will move', etc. We use the same tense in English: 'the battalion will parade . . .'. The usual negative in this jussive use of the future is οὐ, but there are examples of μή, as here.

l. 9. ἀνίσχοντι intransitive, 'rising', ἀνίσχω form of ἀνέχω.

l. 9. ἐν μετώπῳ, 'in line'.

l. 13. ἐκβῶσι, i.e. the Athenians.

l. 14. ἐξεβίβασαν, i.e. τοὺς ναύτας.

l. 17. ἐκ τῶν τειχῶν, i.e. his castle; see Chapter V ad fin.

l. 21. ἐν καλῷ, 'in a good position'. There seems to be something wrong in Xenophon's figures, unless the text is corrupt.

If the Athenians had to go 1⅓ miles for rations, that is no
distance for able-bodied men, though it might entail climbing
the cliffs. Again, if they were only 1⅓ miles from Sestos, they
might as well have been in the harbour, as Alcibiades suggested,
though there was a headland in between to be rounded. But
they must have been considerably more than 15 stades from
Sestos to be anything like opposite Lampsacus, which is about
18 miles from Sestos as the crow flies. If the 180 triremes were
drawn up on the beach only ten feet apart they would occupy
more than a mile.

l. 27. ἐπήν = ἐπεὶ ἄν.

l. 37. δίκροτοι, double-beating, and so 'with two banks of
oars manned'. μανόκροτοι similarly = 'with one bank of oars
manned'. In some of the ships only a proportion of the crew
appear to have gone for rations.

l. 39. ἡ Πάραλος. See introduction to next Chapter.

ll. 44–5. τὰ μεγάλα . . . ἱστία. See Introduction, Section 4,
p. xxxv. Cape Abarnis is a headland to the south of Lampsacus
No doubt the sails were deposited on the beach below, and not
on the cliff top. There would be little time for Conon's men to
climb cliffs and carry down the heavy sails of 200 triremes, and
then stow them on board. They seem to have been most
inadequately guarded, if at all. It was a bold raid, and we
should like to know what Lysander said or thought when he
found out what had happened.

CHAPTER XII. THE NEWS AT ATHENS

Line 1. We are not told how long the Paralus took to reach
Athens. Probably it was the second night after the battle.
A messenger dispatched by Lysander on the day of the battle
(which took place late in the day) reached Sparta τριταῖος, on
the third day. This involved thirty miles overland.

ll. 3–4. ὁ ἕτερος τῷ ἑτέρῳ παραγγέλλων. This nominative
phrase is in apposition to οἰμωγὴ διῆκεν. The unorthodox
grammar is well suited to the dramatic tension of the passage, as
also in the next sentence, where οὐδείς is taken up by πενθοῦντες.

This list of Greek communities which had suffered cruelly at the hands of Athens is well headed by Melos, an island which had never joined the Delian League or formed part of the Athenian empire. Under the influence of Alcibiades it was attacked and besieged. On its surrender in 416 B.C. all men of military age were put to death, the remainder of the inhabitants enslaved, and the island colonised by Athenians. This wanton aggression has been made famous by the prominence given to it in the pages of *Thucydides* (V. 84 ff.), who has made the episode dramatic by constructing a dialogue between the Athenian envoys and the Melians in which the doctrine 'might is right' is shamelessly laid down. The Trojan Women of Euripides was a bitter protest against this episode.

Histiaea, a city in Euboea, which revolted from Athens in 447 B.C. The island was reduced gradually, Histiaea holding out longest. Its citizens were driven out and its territory annexed.

Scione and Torone were both cities in Chalcidice. Torone was captured by Brasidas in 424 B.C., and Scione revolted from Athens in 423 B.C. By the terms of the Peace of Nicias Athens was left a free hand to deal with them. Both were recovered and the male inhabitants put to death. Scione was destroyed.

Aegina was an old commercial rival of Athens. In 431 B.C. Athens seized Aegina to secure her strategic position in the Saronic gulf, drove out the inhabitants, and settled her own citizens there.. In recent times we have seen Russia annex part of Poland and the Baltic states, to secure her position against a German attack in 1939.

l. 13. περὶ ταῦτα ἦσαν: 'were engaged in these matters'.

CHAPTER XIII. THE SURRENDER AND THE PEACE

Lines 1–2. ἔπεμψε . . . ὅτι, 'sent word that . . .'.

ll. 4–5. τοῦ ἑτέρου Λακεδιμονίων βασιλέως. The dual monarchy was a very remarkable feature of the Spartan constitution.

l. 7. ἐν τῇ 'Ακαδημείᾳ τῷ καλουμένῳ γυμνασίῳ, 'in the Academy, as that gymnasium is called'. The Academy was situated in the suburbs of Athens, by the river Cephisus. It became famous when Plato used it as a centre for the teaching of philosophy which he established there about 385 B.C. This college lasted as an institution with a corporate life till as late as A.D. 529. Hence the title academy has been used in many civilized countries for learned or artistic bodies or even for schools. It is one of those strange twists of language that 'academic' should sometimes be used in the sense of 'merely theoretical' or 'unpractical', or almost as a term of abuse when it is derived from the name of a sports ground called after a local hero Academus.

l. 10. τῆς αὐτῶν, i.e. γῆς.

l. 13. τὰ πλοῖα, ships which might have brought much needed supplies of corn.

ll. 16–17. σωτηρίαν τοῦ μὴ παθεῖν, 'security against suffering'. τοῦ is an emendation, but the reading is doubtful.

l. 17. οὐ goes closely with τιμωρούμενοι, 'when they were not avenging themselves', i.e. attacking without provocation.

l. 19. ἐκείνοις, i.e. the Peloponnesians.

ll. 19–20. τοὺς ἀτίμους ἐπιτίμους ποιήσαντες. ἄτιμος is one who having been convicted of some crime has been deprived of civil rights and privileges. This far-reaching amnesty was embodied in a decree proposed by a certain Patroclides, and its object was to promote harmony and morale in the beleaguered city.

l. 28. Σελλασίᾳ, on the frontier of Laconia, some seven or eight miles from Sparta.

l. 29. οἱ ἔφοροι. The ephors, and not the kings, dealt with foreign affairs and matters of peace and war.

ll. 38–9. τῶν μακρῶν τειχῶν, partitive genitive; 'pull down part of the Long Walls for a distance of ten stades of each'.

The Long Walls were built in 461–456 B.C. Originally the south wall included Phalerum, while the north wall ran straight to the Piraeus. In 455 B.C. a third wall was added, parallel to the north wall, and the south wall was not kept in repair. These walls were about 4½ miles long and turned Athens and the Piraeus into a fortified area, into which the inhabitants were brought when Attica was evacuated on the Spartan invasions in 431 B.C. and following years.

l. 41. τοιούτων δὲ ὄντων, i.e. τῶν πραγμάτων.

ll. 45–6. ἐπιτηρῶν ὁπότε, 'waiting for the time when ...'; but we are told above that the corn supply was already exhausted.

l. 50. κύριος ὤν = κύριος τούτων ἅ, relative attraction.

l. 51. πρεσβευτής, an ambassador; for the plural, πρέσβεις (from πρέσβυς) is normally used.

l. 52. δέκατος αὐτός, 'himself the tenth' means 'in command himself with nine colleagues'—a common idiom.

l. 58. καλεῖν, 'gave orders to summon them'.

l. 70. ὄχλος ... φοβούμενοι. Construction according to the sense.

l. 70. ἄπρακτοι, like re infecta in Latin, 'without accomplishing anything'.

l. 77. According to Plutarch, Lysander arrived in Athens on the 16th of the month Munychion, early April, 404 B.C.

VOCABULARY

For principal parts of compound verbs see the simple verb.

ABBREVIATIONS

acc. =accusative	*impers.* =impersonal
adj. =adjective	*intrans.* =intransitive
adv. =adverb	*mid.* =middle
aor. =aorist	*pass.* =passive
conj. =conjunction	*pl.* =plural
dat. =dative	*prep.* =preposition
gen. =genitive	*pron.* =pronoun

α

ἀγγέλλω, ἀγγελῶ, ἤγγειλα, ἤγγελκα, ἠγγέλθην, ἤγγελμαι, announce, report, bring news.

ἄγκυρα, -ας, ἡ, anchor.

ἀγνώς, -ῶτος, unknown.

ἄγω, ἄξω, ἤγαγον, ἦχα, ἤχθην, ἦγμαι, lead, carry, bring, keep, observe (of a feast).

ἀδικέω, treat unjustly, do wrong to, (*intrans.*) act wrongly or unjustly.

ἀεί, *adv.*, always, from time to time.

ἄθλιος, -α, -ον, wretched, miserable.

ἀθροίζω, gather together, collect.

ἄθροος, -α, -ον, sometimes ἄθρους, -ουν, crowded, together, in a body.

ἀθυμέω, be disheartened, despond.

ἀθυμία, -ας, ἡ, lack of spirit, despondency.

αἰγιαλός, -ου, ὁ, shore, beach.

αἰθρία, -ας, ἡ, clear, fine weather.

αἱρέω, αἱρήσω, εἷλον, ᾕρηκα, ᾑρέθην, ᾕρημαι, take, seize; (*mid.*), choose.

αἴρω, ἀρῶ, ἦρα, ἦρκα, ἤρθην, raise; (*intrans.*) get under way.

αἰσθάνομαι, αἰσθήσομαι, ᾐσθόμην, ᾔσθημαι, perceive, notice (+*gen.*)

αἰσχρός, -ά, -όν, ugly, base, shameful.

αἰτέω, ask, ask for, demand.

αἰτιάζομαι, be accused.

αἰτιάομαι, blame, censure, hold responsible, allege as the cause.

αἴτιος, -α, -ον, culpable, responsible for.

ἀκούω, ἀκούσομαι, ἤκουσα, ἀκήκοα, ἠκούσθην, hear (+*acc. of thing; gen. of person*).

ἄκρα, -ας, ἡ, headland, cape.

ἀκρατεία, -ας, ἡ, lack of self-control, wanton behaviour.

ἁλίσκομαι, ἁλώσομαι, ἑάλων, ἑάλωκα, be taken, caught, seized.

ἀλλά, (*conj.*) but.

ἀλλήλους, -ας, -α, one another.

ἄλλοθεν, (*adv.*), from another place.

ἄλλος, -η, -ο, other, another; of time, next.

ἄλφιτον, -ου, τό, (usually in pl.), barley, barley-meal.

ἅμα, (adv.), at once, together; (as prep. +dat.) at the same time with, together with.

ἀμέλεια, -ας, ἡ, carelessness, neglect.

ἀμφότεροι, -αι, -α, both.

ἄν, particle used in certain conditional, potential, and indefinite clauses.

ἄν, contracted form of ἐάν.

ἀνα-βαίνω, -βήσομαι, -εβην, -βέβηκα, go up, mount, go inland, mount the rostrum, i.e. come forward to speak.

ἀνα-βάλλω, -βαλῶ, -έβαλον, -βέβληκα, -εβλήθην, -βέβλημαι, put back, put off; (esp. in mid.), delay, adjourn.

ἀναβολή, -ῆς, ἡ, delay.

ἀν-άγω, lead up, raise, take inland, take to sea; (mid. and pass.) put out to sea, set sail.

ἀναγκάζω, compel.

ἀνάγκη, -ης, ἡ, necessity, compulsion.

ἀναγωγή, -ῆς, ἡ, a putting out to sea, setting sail.

ἀνα-δέω, bind, fasten up; (mid.) take in tow.

ἀναίρεσις, -εως, ἡ, taking up.

ἀν-αιρέω, take up, rescue (also mid.).

ἀνα-λαμβάνω, take up.

ἀναλίσκω, ἀναλώσω, ἀνήλωσα, ἀνήλωκα, ἀνηλώθην, ἀνήλωμαι, spend.

ἀνα-παύω, make to stop; (mid. and pass.), rest.

ἀναρρηθῆναι (aor. pass. infin. of ἀνεῖπον), announce, proclaim.

ἀνδραποδίζω, enslave.

ἀν-έλκω, -έλξω, -είλκυσα, -ειλκύσθην, -είλκυσμαι, draw up, beach.

ἄνεμος, -ου, ὁ, wind.

ἀνεπιτήδειος, -ον, unserviceable, unfit, ill-omened.

ἀν-έχω, hold up, lift up; (intrans.) rise, wait, cease; (mid.) endure, put up with.

ἀνεψιός, -οῦ, ὁ, cousin.

ἀνήρ, ἀνδρός, ὁ, man.

ἄνθρωπος, -ου, ὁ, man, human being.

ἀν-ίστημι, raise, set up; (intrans.) rise.

ἀν-οίγνυμι, -οίξω, -έῳξα, -εῴχθην, -εῴγμαι, open, open up; (intrans.) get into open sea, get clear of land.

ἀνταν-άγω, lead up against; take out to sea against; (mid.) put out to sea against.

ἀντ-έχω, hold out against, withstand, endure.

ἀντι-λέγω, λέξω, ἀντεῖπον, speak against.

ἀντίον, opposite, against; (as prep. + gen.), opposite to.

ἀντι-τάττω, draw up against, range against.

ἀνυπόδητος, -ον, unshod, without shoes.

ἀπ-αγγέλλω, bring back news, report.

ἀπ-άγω, lead away; (intrans.), withdraw.

ἀπ-αντάω, meet.

ἅπας, ἅπασα, ἅπαν, all, all together.

ἀπειλέω, keep away (see note on ch. I, l. 29).

ἄπ-ειμι (εἰμί be), away from, far from, absent.

ἄπ-ειμι (εἶμι go), go away, depart.

ἄπειρος, -ον, inexperienced.

ἀπ-έρχομαι, go away, depart.

ἀπό (prep. +gen.), from, away from; used of place, time, origin or cause.

ἀπο-βαίνω, go away, disembark, result.

ἀπο-βιβάζω, disembark, put on shore.

ἀπο-διδράσκω, -δράσομαι, -έδραν, -δέδρακα, run away, escape.

ἀπο-δίδωμι, give back, deliver, refer, pay; (mid.) sell.

ἀπο-θνησκω, -θανοῦμαι, ἀπέθανον, τέθνηκα, die; (often in pass. sense) be killed.

ἄποικος, -ου, ὁ, settler, colonist.

ἀπο-κόπτω, cut off, sever.

ἀπο-κρίνομαι, -κρινοῦμαι, -εκρινάμην, answer.

ἀπο-κτείνω, -κτενῶ, -έκτεινα, kill.

ἀπο-λείπω, leave, desert.

ἀπ-όλλυμι, -ολῶ, -ώλεσα, -ολώλεκα, -ωλόμην, -όλωλα, destroy, lose; (mid.) perish.

ἀπολόγεομαι, speak in defence, defend oneself.

ἀπο-πίπτω, -πεσοῦμαι, -έπεσον, -πέπτωκα, fall off.

ἀπο-πλέω, sail away.

ἀπορέω, be at a loss, in difficulties, in want of.

ἀπόρως (adv.), at a loss, in difficulties.

ἀποσεύω, chase away; ἀπεσσύθη (aor. pass.), run away, vanish. (see note on ch. I.)

ἀπο-φεύγω, flee from, escape.

ἀπο-χώννυμι (aor., έχωσα), bank up, block up.

ἄπρακτος, -ον, unavailing, unsuccessful.

ἀπροθύμως, unreadily, without enthusiasm.

ἅπτομαι, touch, fasten on (+gen.).

ἀργύριον, -ου, τό, coin, piece of money, money.

ἀργυρολογέω, collect money.

ἀργυροῦς, ᾶ, οῦν (ἀργύρεος), of silver.

ἀρέσκω, ἀρέσω, ἤρεσα, please, satisfy; ἀρέσκει, (impers.) it is approved, decided.

ἄριστα, adv. of ἄριστος.

ἀριστερός, ά, όν, left, on the left; ἡ ἀριστερά, left hand.

ἄριστον, -ου, τό, breakfast, morning meal.

ἀριστοποιέω, prepare breakfast; (mid.), take breakfast.

ἄριστος, η, ον (superl. of ἀγαθός), best.

ἀρκέω, ἀρκέσω, ἤρκεσα, suffice, avail.

ἄρτι (adv.), lately, just now.

ἄρχω, begin, lead, be in command, be a magistrate or archon.

ἀσεβέω, act impiously, commit sacrilege.

ἀσπίς, -ιδος, ἡ, shield.

ἄστυ, -εως, τό, town.

ἄτιμος, -ον, unhonoured, dishonourable, deprived of, or without civic rights.

αὖ (adv.), again, on the other hand.

αὖθις (adv.), again.

αὐλητρίς, -ίδος, ἡ, flute-girl.

αὐλίζομαι, (aor., ηὐλισάμην and ηὐλίσθην), bivouac, lodge, pass the night.

αὐτόθεν (adv.), from the very place, from there, immediately.

αὐτόθι (adv.), on the spot, there.

αὐτοκράτωρ, -ορος, with full powers, in chief command.

αὐτός,ή,ό (adj.), self, emphasising person, myself, himself, itself, etc.; ὁ αὐτός, the same (in oblique cases used as 3rd pers. pron.).
αὐτοῦ = ἑαυτοῦ.
αὐτοῦ (adv.), there, where he, they, etc., were.
αὕτως (adv.),. in the very manner; ὡσαύτως (sometimes separated by δέ-ὡς δ' αὕτως), in the same manner.
ἀφανίζω, make to disappear; (pass.) disappear, be missing.
ἄφθονος, -ον, ungrudging, ungrudged, plentiful, abundant.
ἀφ-ίημι, send forth, send away, let go, leave, neglect.
ἀφικνέομαι, ἀφίξομαι, ἀφικόμην, ἀφῖγμαι, arrive.
ἀφ-ίστημι, remove, put away, cause to revolt; (mid.) stand aloof from, revolt.
ἀφ-ορμάω, make to start; (intrans. and pass.) start, depart.
ἄχθομαι, ἀχθέσομαι, ἠχθέσθην, ἤχθεσομαι, be vexed, angry.

β

βαίνω, βήσομαι, ἔβην, βέβηκα, go.
βάλλω, βαλῶ, ἔβαλον, βέβληκα, ἐβλήθην, βέβλημαι, throw, hit.
βάρβαρcς, -ον, barbarian, non-Greek, foreign.
βασιλεύς, -έως, ὁ, king; (without the article) king of Persia.
βέλτιον (adv. of βελτίων), better.
βλάπτω, damage, hurt.
βοάω, shout, cry aloud.
βοήθεια, -ας, ἡ, help.
βοηθέω, help, come to the rescue.
βουλεύω, plan, devise; (mid.) deliberate, resolve.

βουλή, -ῆς, ἡ, counsel, design, council (esp. of the Council of 500 at Athens).
βούλομαι, βουλήσομαι, ἐβουλήθην (augment in imperf. and aor., ἐ or ἠ) wish, profess, claim.
βραχέως (adv.), shortly.
βροντή, -ῆς, ἡ, thunder.

γ

γάρ (conj.), for.
γῆ, γῆς, ἡ, earth, land.
γίγνομαι, γενήσομαι, ἐγενόμην, γέγονα and γεγένημαι, become, happen, show oneself or behave; (in a pass. sense) be made, be appointed.
γιγνώσκω, γνώσομαι, ἔγνων, ἔγνωκα get to know, learn, determine, think.
γνώμη, -ης, ἡ, thought, judgment, decision, opinion, motion.
γράμμα, -ατος, τό, written character, letter; (in pl.) piece of writing, letter, document.
γράφω, γράψω, ἔγραψα, γέγραφα, ἐγράφην, γέγραμμαι, write, propose.
γυμνάζω, train, exercise.
γυμνάσιον, -ου, τό, gymnasium, training-ground, sports ground.
γυμνός, -ή, -όν, naked, bare, lightly or poorly clad.

δ

δέ conj.), and, but (in the second of a pair of clauses, see μέν).
δέδια (perf. with pres. meaning), fear.
δεῖ, (impers.), it is necessary, it behoves (+acc. and infin.).

δεινός, -ή, -όν, strange, dreadful, clever, skilful.

δεῖπνον, -ου, τό, dinner, evening meal.

δειπνοποιέω, prepare dinner; (mid.) take dinner, dine.

δέκα, ten.

δεκατευτήριον, -ου, τό, office for collection of tithes, customs duties, custom-house.

δέκατος, -η, -ον, tenth; δεκάτη, -ης. ἡ (i.e. μέρις), tenth part, tithe, customs duty of one tenth.

δεξιός; ά, -όν, on the right hand or side, right.

δέχομαι, receive, accept.

δέω (I), δήσω, ἔδησα, δέδεκα, ἐδέθην, δέδεγμαι, bind, fasten, imprison.

δέω (II), δεήσω, ἐδέησα, lack, need; (mid.) want, beg, ask for (+gen.).

δή (adv.), indeed.

δῆμος, -ου, ὁ, the people, the commons, democratic party, democracy.

δηόω, lay waste, ravage.

διά (prep. +acc.), on account of; (+gen.) through.

δια-βιβάζω, take over, lead across, transport.

διαβολή, -ῆς, ἡ, false accusation, slander.

δια-δίδωμι, hand over, distribute.

δια-θροέω, spread a report.

διακόσιοι, -αι, -α, two hundred.

δια-κωλύω, prevent, hinder.

δια-λέγομαι, discuss, converse with (+dat.).

διαλλαγή, -ῆς, ἡ, reconciliation.

δι-αλλάττω, change, exchange, reconcile.

δια-πλέω, sail through.

δια-σκεδάννυμι, scatter abroad.

δια-σπείρω, -οπερῶ, -έσπειρα, -ἐσπάρην, -ἐσπαρμαι, scatter abroad, disperse.

δια-τρίβω, rub away, consume, spend, delay.

δια-φεύγω, get away, escape.

δια-φθείρω, -φθερῶ, -ἐφθειρα, -ἐφθαρκα, -ἐφθάρην, -ἐφθαρμαι, destroy utterly.

δια-φυλάττω, watch closely.

δια-χειροτονέω, choose, elect, select.

διαχειροτονία, -ας, ἡ, choice, election.

διαψήφισις, -εως, ἡ, voting.

διδάσκω, instruct, teach.

δίδωμι, δώσω, ἔδωκα, δέδωκα, ἐδόθην, δέδομαι. give.

διέκπλους, -ου, ὁ, diecplus, breaking the enemy's line (see Introduction, § 4).

δι-έχω, keep apart; (intrans.) be apart, distant, wide.

δι-ηγέομαι, set out in detail, describe, recount.

δι-ήκω, extend, reach, pervade.

δίκαιος, -α, -ον, just, right, lawful; + εἶναι, be bound to, have a right to.

δικαστήριον, ου, τό, law-court, court of justice.

δίκροτος, -ον, with two banks of oars manned, with two squads of rowers.

δίοτι (conj.), because, for the reason that, for what reason.

δίχα (adv.), apart, separately.

διωβελία, ας, ἡ, allowance of two obols a day (at Athens, see note).

διώκω, pursue, follow closely.

δοκέω, think, seem; (impers.) δοκεῖ, it seems good, it is resolved.

δραχμή, -ῆς, ἡ, drachma, silver coin worth six obols.

δράω, do.

δύναμαι, δυνήσομαι, ἐδυνήθην, δεδύνημαι, be able, have the power.

δύναμις, -εως, ἡ, strength, power, influence.

δυνατός, -ή, -όν, strong, able, possible.

δύνω, also δύω, sink, set.

δύο, two.

δύσνους, -ουν, ill-affected, disaffected.

ε

ἐάν (conj.), also, ἄν, if (only with subj.).

ἐαυτόν, -ήν, -ό (3rd pers. refl. pron.) himself, etc; also αὐτόν, etc.

ἐάω, ἐάσω, εἴασα, allow.

ἐβδομήκοντα, seventy.

ἐγγυάω, give a pledge; (mid.) pledge oneself, give security.

ἐγγυητής, -οῦ, ὁ, one who has given security, guarantor.

ἐγγύς (adv.), near (as prep. +gen.).

ἐγείρω, awake, arouse; (pass.) wake, arouse oneself.

ἐγκατα-λείπω, leave behind.

ἐγχειρίδιον, -ου, τό, dagger.

ἐγ-χωρέω, allow; (impers.), ἐγχωρεῖ, it is allowed, permissible, there is time.

ἐγώ (pron.), I.

ἕδος, -ους, τό, seat, abode, statue.

εἰ (conj.), if, whether.

εἴκοσι(ν), twenty.

εἰμί, ἔσομαι, be.

εἶμι, will go, go (used as fut. of ἔρχομαι).

εἶπον (used as aor. of λέγω), say.

εἴργω, shut in or out, prevent.

εἰρήνη, -ης, ἡ, peace.

εἰς (prep. +acc.), to, towards, into.

εἷς, μία, ἕν, one.

εἰσ-βαίνω, -βήσομαι, -εβην, -βέβηκα, enter, go on board, embark.

εἰσ-δέχομαι, take into, admit.

εἴσ-ειμι (εἶμι, go), go into, enter.

εἰσ-πλέω, sail into.

εἴσπλους, -ου, ὁ, sailing in.

εἰσ-τίθημι, put into, put on board ship.

εἶτα (adv.), then, next.

εἴτε ... εἴτε (conj.), whether ... or (in alternative conditions).

εἰσ-φέρω, bring in, contribute, introduce, propose.

ἐκ, ἐξ (prep. +gen.), from, out of.

ἕκαστος, -η, -ον, each; (pl.) each group or party.

ἑκάτερος, -α, -ον, each of two.

ἑκατόν, the hundred.

ἐκ-βιβάζω, make to go out, land, disemdark.

ἐκ-βοηθέω, march out to aid, sally.

ἐκεῖ (adv.), there, in that place.

ἐκεῖθεν (adv.), thence, from that place, from there.

ἐκεῖνος, -η, -ο (adj. and pron.), that, he, she, etc.

ἐκεῖσε (adv.), thither, to that place, there.

ἐκκλησία, -ας, ἡ, assembly, meeting (esp. of the assembly at Athens).

ἐκ-λάμπω, shine out, shine forth.

ἐκ-λέγω, pick out, levy (taxes, etc.).

ἐκ-λείπω, leave out, abandon; (intrans.) be eclipsed.

ἐκ-πέμπω, send out.

ἐκ-πλέω, sail out, sail away.

ἔκπλους, -ου, ὁ, sailing out, passage out, exit (from a harbour).

ἐκτός (prep. +gen.), without, outside, except.

ἐκ-φεύγω, escape.

ἐλαττόω, make less, reduce; (pass.) be inferior.

ἐλευθερία, -ας, ἡ, freedom, liberty.

ἐμ-βάλλω, throw in; (intrans.), attack, invade, ram.

ἔμπαλιν (adv.), back, backwards.

ἔμπειρος, -ον, experienced.

ἐμ-πίμπρημι, -πρήσω, -έπρησα, -επρήσθην, set on fire, burn down.

ἐμ-πίπτω, fall upon, attack.

ἐμφανής, -ές, visible, manifest; ἐκ τοῦ ἐμφανοῦς, clearly, openly.

ἐν (prep. +dat.), in.

ἐναντίος, -α, -ον, opposite, opposing, hostile.

ἕνεκα (also ἕνεκεν, prep. +gen.), on account of, for the sake of, as regards.

ἐνθάδε (adv.), here.

ἔνιοι, -αι, -α, some.

ἐννέα, nine.

ἐνταῦθα (adv.), here, there, then, thereupon.

ἐντεῦθεν (adv.), thence, thereupon.

ἐν-τυγχάνω, meet, meet with (+ dat.).

ἐξ (prep.), see ἐκ.

ἕξ, six.

ἐξ-αγγέλλω, tell out, report, proclaim.

ἐξ-άγω, lead out, bring out.

ἐξ-αιρέω, take out, remove, destroy; (mid.) take out for oneself, remove.

ἐξ-ανδραποδίζω (usually mid.) reduce to complete slavery, enslave.

ἐξ-απατάω, deceive.

ἐξαπιναίως (adv.), suddenly.

ἔξ-ειμι (εἶμι, go), go out.

ἔξεστι(ν) (impers.), it is permitted, is possible.

ἑξήκοντα, sixty.

ἔξω (adv.), outside; (prep. +gen.) outside.

ἑορτή, -ῆς, ἡ, feast, festival.

ἐπ-αινέω, praise, approve, commend, thank.

ἐπακτρίς, -ίδος, ἡ, light vessel, pinnace.

ἐπαν-άγω, lead up, bring back, take out to sea against; (pass.) put out to sea against.

ἐπανα-φέρω, bring back, report, refer.

ἐπαν-ίστημι, set up again, cause to revolt; (intrans. and mid.) rise up against, arise.

ἐπεί (conj.), when, since.

ἐπειδάν (conj.), whenever (+subj.).

ἐπειδή (conj.), when, since.

ἔπειμι (εἶμι, go), come upon, attack; (particip., ἐπιών, of time), following.

ἐπεισ-πλέω, sail in after.

ἐπ-έχω, hold out, present, keep in check, aim at, attack; (intrans.) stay, pause, cease from.

ἐπήν for ἐπεὶ ἄν.

ἐπί (prep. +acc.), to, against, for; (+gen.) towards, upon, ἐπὶ μιᾶς, in one row, one deep;

VOCABULARY 59

(+dat.) upon, on condition of, over, behind.

ἐπι-βάλλω, throw upon, impose.

ἐπιβάτης, -ου, ὁ, soldier serving on ship, marine.

ἐπιβολή, -ῆς, ἡ, penalty, fine.

ἐπι-γίγνομαι, come upon, come after.

ἐπι-δείκνυμι. -δείξω, -έδειξα, show, exhibit.

ἐπι-θορυβέω, shout aloud (displeasure or approval).

ἐπι-κηρύττω, proclaim, declare.

ἐπι-λείπω, leave; (intrans.), fail.

ἐπι-μελέομαι, also, ἐπι-μέλομαι, take care of, take charge of (+gen.).

ἐπι-πλέω, sail against.

ἐπίπλους, -ου, ὁ, sailing against, attack by sea.

ἐπι-σιτίζομαι, obtain supplies (of food).

ἐπι-στέλλω, command, give orders.

ἐπιστολεύς, -έως, ὁ, second-in-command of the Spartan navy.

ἐπιστολή, -ῆς, ἡ, letter.

ἐπι-τάττω, place next or behind, command.

ἐπιτήδειος, -α, -ον, fit, suitable, necessary, friendly; (as noun) friend; τὰ ἐπιτήδεια, necessaries, provisions.

ἐπι-τηρέω, watch for.

ἐπι-τίθημι, place upon; (mid.), attack.

ἐπίτιμος, -ον, in possession of one's rights, enfranchized.

ἐπι-τρέπω, entrust, leave to, permit, allow.

ἐπι-χειρέω, put one's hand to, attempt.

ἕπομαι, ἕψομαι, ἑσπόμην, follow (+ dat.).

ἑπτά, seven.

ἐργάζομαι, work, labour, perform.

ἔργον, -ου, τό, work, deed.

ἐρέτης, -ου, ὁ, oarsman, rower.

ἔρομαι, ἐρήσομαι, ἠρόμην, ask.

ἔρρω, come to harm, be lost, perish.

ἐρῶ (used as fut. of λέγω), say.

ἔρχομαι, ἐλεύσομαι, ἦλθον, ἐλήλυθα, come, go.

ἐρωτάω, ask.

ἑσπέρα, -ας, ἡ, evening.

ἕτερος, -α, -ον, the other (of two).

ἔτι (adv.), still, yet, further.

ἔτος, -ους, τό, year.

εὐθέως (adv.), immediately.

εὐθύ (prep. +gen.), straight for.

εὐθύς (adv.), immediately.

εὔνους, -ουν, well-disposed, friendly.

εὐπορέω (+gen.), have plenty of, abound in.

εὐτρεπίζω, make ready, prepare.

εὐώνυμος, -ον, left, on the left hand; τὸ εὐώνυμον, the left.

ἐφ-ίστημι, set over; (intrans. and mid.) stand near.

ἐφόδιον, -ου, τό, supplies, maintenance.

ἐφορεύω, be ephor, serve as ephor (at Sparta).

ἐφορμέω, lie moored at, (blockade).

ἔφορος, -ου, ὁ, ephor (Spartan magistrate).

ἐχθρός, -ά, -όν, hateful, hating, hostile; (as noun) the enemy.

ἔχω, ἕξω, σχήσω, ἔσχον, ἔσχηκα, have, hold; σχήσω, ἔσχον, get; (+adv.), be; (mid.) cling to, be close to.

ἕως (conj.), while, until.

ζ

ζημία, -ας, ἡ, loss, damage, penalty.
ζωγρέω, take alive, capture.

η

ἤ (conj.), or; ἤ ... ἤ, either ... or.
ᾗ (adv.), where, by which way.
ἡγεμών, -όνος, ὁ, leader.
ἡγέομαι, lead (+ dat.), command, regard, think.
ἤδη (adv.), already, now.
ἥκω, have come, have arrived.
ἥλιος, -ου, ὁ, sun.
ἡμεῖς (pron.), we.
ἡμέρα, -ας, ἡ, day.

θ

θάλαττα, -ης, ἡ, sea.
θαλαττοκρατέω, be master of the sea, be supreme at sea, rule the waves.
θαλαττοκράτωρ, -ορος, ὁ, master of the sea, supreme at sea.
θάνατος, -ου, ὁ, death.
θαυμάζω, wonder, wonder at, admire, reverence.
θέρος, -ους, τό, summer.
θόρυβος, -ου, ὁ, noise, tumult, confusion.
θρόνος, -ου, ὁ, throne, chair of state.
θύρα, -ας, ἡ, door.

ι

ἰατρεῖον, -ου, τό, surgery.
ἰδίᾳ (adv.), privately.
ἴδιος, -α, -ον, private, one's own.
ἰδιώτης, -ου, ὁ, private person, individual.
ἵημι, ἥσω, ἧκα, εἷκα, εἵθην, εἷμα:, send, let go.

ἱκανός, -ή, -όν, sufficient, competent, adequate.
ἱμάτιον, -ου, τό, cloak, outer garment.
ἱππεύς, -έως, ὁ, horseman; (pl.) cavalry.
ἴσος, -η, -ον, equal.
ἵστημι, στήσω, ἔστησα, ἔστην (intrans.) ἔστηκα (intrans.), ἐστάθην, ἔσταμαι, make to stand, set up; (intrans and pass.) stand, stand still, halt.
ἱστίον, -ου, τό, sail.

κ

καθαίρεσις, -εως, ἡ, pulling down, demolition.
καθ-αιρέω, pull down, demolish, destroy.
καθ-άπτω, fasten upon; (mid.) attach blame to, upbraid (+ gen.).
καθ-έλκω, drag down, launch.
κάθημαι, sit, sit down.
καθ-ίημι, send down, let down, allow to return, restore.
καθ-ίστημι, place, establish, ordain; (intrans., mid. and pass.) settle, become, be established, prevail; τὰ καθεστῶτα, the existing situation.
καθ-οράω, look down on, see clearly, spot.
καί (conj. and adv.), and, also, even; καί ... καί and ... τε καί ..., both ... and.
κάκιον, compar. of κακῶς.
κακός, -ή, -ον, bad, evil, τὸ κακόν, evil, misfortune.
κακῶς (adv.), ill, evilly, badly.
καλαμηφόρος, -ον: carrying a reed or straw.

κάλαμος, -ου, ὁ, reed or straw.

καλέω, καλέσω or καλῶ, ἐκάλεσα, κέκληκα, ἐκλήθην, κέκλημαι, call, summon.

καλλίων, compar. of καλός.

καλός, -ή, -όν, beautiful, good; ἐν καλῷ, in a good place; τὰ καλά, success, good fortune.

καλῶς (adv.), well, fairly.

καρτερέω, endure, be steadfast.

κατά (prep. +acc.), down, along, according to, throughout; (+gen.) down from, down into, against.

κατάδηλος, -ον, manifest, clear, visible.

κατα-δύω sink; (intrans.) become water-logged.

κατα-θέω, run down, run into port.

κατα-καίω, -καύσω, -έκαυσα, burn completely, burn up.

κατα-καλύπτω, cover up.

κατα-κλείω, shut in, enclose.

κατα-κόπτω, cut down, coin into money.

κατα-κωλύω, hinder.

κατα-λαμβάνω, seize, overtake, come upon, find.

κατα-λέγω, recount, reckon up, enrol.

κατα-λείπω, leave behind.

κατα-μανθάνω, observe, perceive.

κατα-πλέω, sail to land, put in.

κατάπλους, -ου, ὁ, sailing to land, putting in, voyage home.

κατα-σκάπτω, dig down, raze to the ground.

κατα-σκευάζω, equip, furnish.

κατασκοπή, -ῆς, ἡ, viewing closely, spying.

κατα-στασιάζω, oppose or overpower by a faction.

κατα-στρέφω, overturn; (mid.) subdue.

κατάστρωμα, -ατος, τό, deck.

κατα-φρονέω, despise.

κατα-ψηφίζομαι, vote against, vote to condemn.

κάτ-ειμι (εἶμι, go), go down, return.

κατ-έρχομαι, come down, return, return from exile.

κατ-έχω, hold, detain, occupy; (intrans.) sail to land, put in.

κατ-ηγορέω, accuse.

κείρω, (perf. mid.) κέκαρμαι, cut the hair, shave; (mid.) cut one's hair.

κελεύω, order, command.

κενός, -ή, -όν, empty.

κέρας, -ατος, τό, horn, wing, flank.

κινδυνεύω, be in danger, risk.

κίνδυνος, -ου, ὁ, danger.

κινέω, set in motion, move; (pass.) move, stir.

κλῆσις, -εως, ἡ, summons, prosecution.

κοῖλος, -η, -ον, hollow; κοίλη ναῦς, the hold.

κοιμάω, put to sleep; (mid. and pass.) fall asleep.

κολακεύω, flatter.

κόλπος, -ου, ὁ, fold, bay, gulf.

κομίζω, carry, convey; (mid.) recover.

κρατέω be powerful, prevail, conquer; (+gen.) get possession of, get the mastery over.

κράτιστα adv. of κράτιστος.

κράτιστος, -η, -ον, strongest, best (used as superl. of ἀγαθός, good).

κράτος, -ους, τό, strength, power; κατὰ κράτος, with all one's might.

κρίνω, choose, decide, judge, bring to trial.

κυβερνάω, be helmsman, steer.

κυβερνήτης, -ου, ὁ, helmsman, steersman.

κύριος, -α, -ον, having authority, responsible for; (as noun) lord, master.

κωλύω, prevent, hinder.

λ

λαμβάνω, λήψομαι, ἔλαβον, εἴληφα, ἐλήφθην, εἴλημμαι, take, seize, receive.

λέγω, λέξω, ἔλεξα, ἐλέχθην, εἴλεγμαι, say, speak, tell, (fut. also ἐρῶ, aor. εἶπον, perf. εἴρηκα).

λείπω, λείψω, ἔλιπον, λέλοιπα, ἐλείφθην, λέλειμμαι, leave.

λιμήν, -ένος, ὁ, harbour.

λιμός, -οῦ, ὁ, hunger, famine.

λόγος, -ου, ὁ, word, speech, account, reason.

λοιπός, -ή, -όν, left, remaining.

μ

μάλιστα (adv., superl. of μάλα), most, very much.

μᾶλλον (adv., compar. of μάλα), more, rather.

μανθάνω, μαθήσομαι, ἔμαθον, μεμάθηκα, learn, notice.

μαρτύριον, -ου, τό, evidence, proof, testimony.

μάρτυς, -υρος, ὁ, witness.

μάχομαι, μαχοῦμαι, ἐμαχεσάμην, μεμάχημαι fight (+ dat.).

μέγας, μεγάλη, μέγα, great.

μέγεθος, -ους, τό, greatness, size.

μέγιστα (superl. adv. of μέγας), very greatly, very much.

μεθ-ίστημι, change; (pass. and intrans. tenses) change, change one's position, revolt.

μεθ-ορμίζω, remove to another anchorage, change station.

μείων (used as compar. of ὀλίγος or μικρός), less.

μέλας, μέλαινα, μέλαν, black.

μέλλω, μελλήσω, ἐμέλλησα, (augment sometimes ἠ-), be likely to, sure to, intend, delay.

μέν (part.), indeed, on the one hand, answered by δέ; μὲν οὖν, so then, well then.

μένω, μενῶ, ἔμεινα, remain, wait, wait for.

μέρος, -ους, τό, share, part; ἐν μέρει, in turn.

μέσος, -η, -ον middle, τὸ μέσον, the centre.

μετά (prep. + acc.), after; (+ gen.) with.

μετα-βιβάζω, carry over, transfer.

μεταμέλει (impers., repent (+ dat.)

μετα-πέμπω, send for.

μέτ-ειμι (εἶμι, go) go after, follow, to fetch.

μέτριος, -α, -ον, moderate.

μέτωπον, -ου, τό, forehead, front; ἐν μετώπῳ, in line.

μέχρι (prep. + gen.), as far as, until; (conj.) until (often μέχρι οὗ).

μή (adv.), not, lest (+ verbs of fearing, etc.).

μηδέ (conj.), and not, not even.

μηδείς, μηδεμία, μηδέν, not one, nobody.

μήν, μηνός, ὁ, month.

μικροπολίτης, -ου, ὁ, citizen of a petty state.

μικρός, -ά, -όν, small, little.

μισέω, hate.

μισθός, -οῦ, ὁ, pay, hire, reward.

μνᾶ, μνᾶς, ἡ, mina—coin worth 100 drachmas.

μονόκροτος, with one bank of oars manned, with one squad of rowers.

μόνον (adv.), only.

μυστήρια, -ων, τά, mysteries, secret rites.

ν

ναυαγός, -ον, shipwrecked.

ναυαρχία, -as, ἡ command of a fleet, period of command at sea.

ναύαρχος, -ου, ὁ, commander of a fleet, admiral (esp. of the Spartan commander-in-chief).

ναυμαχέω, fight at sea, engage in naval battle.

ναυμαχία, -as, ἡ, sea-fight, naval battle.

ναυπηγέω, build ships.

ναῦς, νεώς, ἡ, ship.

ναύτης, -ου, ὁ, seaman, sailor.

ναυτικός, -ή, -όν, naval, seafaring; τὸ ναυτικόν, fleet, navy; τὰ ναυτικά, naval matters.

νεώς, νεώ, ὁ, temple, shrine.

νεωτερίζω, make innovations, political movements, revolutions.

νικάω, conquer.

νομίζω, practise, think, consider; (pass.) be customary.

νόμος, -ου, ὁ, law, custom.

νύξ, νυκτός. ἡ, night.

ξ

ξύλον, -ου, τό wood, log, piece of timber.

ο

ὁ, ἡ, τό, (definite article), the; ὁ μέν . . . ὁ δέ, the one . . . the other.

ὀβολός, -οῦ, ὁ, obol, small silver coin (six obols = one drachma).

ὀγδοήκοντα, eighty.

ὅδε, ἥδε, τόδε, this.

ὅθεν (adv.), whence, from which place.

οἶδα, εἴσομαι, ᾔδειν; (infin. εἰδέναι, part. εἰδώς), know.

οἴκαδε (adv.), homewards, home.

οἰκεῖος, -a, -ον, belonging to oneself, one's own.

οἰκέω, inhabit, manage; (intrans.) live, dwell.

οἴκοθεν (adv.), from home.

οἴκοι (adv.), at home.

οἶκος, -ου, ὁ, house, home; οἱ ἐν οἴκῳ, those at home.

οἰμωγή, -ῆς, ἡ, wailing, lamentation.

οἴομαι (οἶμαι), ᾠόμην, think.

οἶος, -a, -ον, what kind of; οἷός τε, able, possible.

οἷοσπερ, οἷαπερ, οἷονπερ, just such as.

οἴχομαι, be gone.

οἰωνίζομαι, take omens, regard as an omen.

ὀκτώ, eight.

ὀλίγος, -η, -ον, small; (in pl.) few.

ὀλιγώρως, carelessly, negligently.

ὁμολογέω, agree, admit.

ὄνομα, -ατος, τό, name.

ὁπλίζω, arm, get ready; (mid. and pass.) arm oneself, get oneself ready.

ὁπλίτης, -ου, ὁ, heavy-armed infantry soldier, hoplite.

ὅπλον, -ου, τό, arm, weapon, tackle; τὰ ὅπλα, the place where arms were kept, camp.

ὅποσος, -η, -ον, as great as, as many as, how many.

ὅποτε (aor.), when.

ὅπως (conj. and adv.), as, how, in order that.

ὁράω, ὄψομαι, εἶδον, ἑώρακα, ὤφθην, see.

ὀργίζομαι, be angry (+dat.).

ὄρθρος, -ου, ὁ, dawn.

ὁρμάω, start, rush (also mid. and pass.).

ὁρμέω, be at anchor.

ὁρμίζω, moor, anchor; (mid. and pass.) lie at anchor.

ὅς, ἥ, ὅ, who, which.

ὅσος, -η, -ον, how great, as great as, as many as.

ὅσπερ, ἥπερ, ὅπερ, exactly who, which.

ὅστις, ἥτις, ὅ τι, who, anyone who, whoever.

ὅταν (conj.), whenever (+ subj.).

ὅτε (conj.), when.

ὅτι (conj.), that, because.

οὐ, οὐκ, οὐχ (adv.), not.

οὗ (adv.), where.

οὐδαμόθεν (adv.), from nowhere, from no side.

οὐδείς, οὐδεμία, οὐδέν, no-one, none.

οὖν (conj.), therefore.

οὗτος, αὕτη, τοῦτο, this.

οὕτως (adv.), thus, so.

ὄφελος, τό, help, advantage.

ὀφθαλμιάω, suffer from ophthalmia, eye-trouble.

ὄχλος, -ου, ὁ, crowd, mob.

ὀψέ (adv.), late.

π

παλαιός, -ά, -όν, old, ancient.

πάλιν (adv.), back, again.

πανδημεί (adv.), with the whole people, in a body, in full force.

παντελῶς (adv.), entirely, utterly,

παρά (prep. +acc.), to, along, contrary to;
(+gen.) from;
(+dat.) at, by the side of.

παρα-βάλλω, place beside, throw over, spread.

παράβλημα, -ατος, τό, screen, awning.

παραγγελλία, -ας, ἡ, command, summons.

παρ-αγγέλλω, pass word, give orders.

παρα-δίδωμι, hand over.

παραθαλάττιος, -α, -ον, beside the sea.

παρα-θαρρύνω, encourage.

παρ-αινέω, exhort, advise.

παρα-κελεύομαι, advise, exhort, encourage (+dat.).

παράνομος, -ον, unlawful, illegal, unconstitutional.

παρα-πίπτω, fall beside, fall in one's way, befall, go astray, blunder.

παρα-πλέω, sail past.

παράρρυμα, -ατος, τό, screen, curtain.

παρα-σκευάζω, get ready, provide; (mid.) prepare oneself.

παρα-τάττω, draw up in battle order, deploy.

πάρ-ειμι (εἰμί, be), be present.

παρ-έρχομαι, pass, come forward to speak.

παρ-έχω, hand over, supply; (mid.) supply from one's own resources.

πᾶς, πᾶσα, πᾶν, all, every.
πάσχω, πείσομαι, ἔπαθον, πέπονθα, suffer.
πατήρ, -τρος, ὁ, father.
πατρίς, -ίδος, ἡ, native land, one's own country.
παύω, make to stop, depose; (mid.) cease.
πεζῇ (adv.), on foot, by land.
πεζομαχέω, light on foot, on land.
πεζός, -ή. -όν, on foot; οἱ πεζοί, infantry; τὸ πεζόν, land-force.
πείθω, persuade; (mid.) obey, trust.
πεινάω, be hungry, starve.
πέλαγος, -ους, τό, sea, the open sea.
πέμπτος, -η, -ον, fifth.
πέμπω, send.
πενθέω, lament, mourn for.
πεντακόσιοι, -αι, -α, five hundred.
πέντε, five.
πειτεκαίδεκα, fifteen.
πεντήκοντα, fifty.
πέραν (adv.), on the other side, opposite.
περί (prep. +acc.), around, about, concerned with; οἱ περὶ + name, so-and-so and his following; (+gen.) concerning.
περι-αιρέω, take from around, remove.
περι-έχω, hold round; (mid.), cling to (+gen.).
περι-πλέω, sail round.
περίπλους, -ου, ὁ, sailing round (esp. of a fleet surrounding the enemy).
πίπτω, πεσοῦμαι, ἔπεσον, πέπτωκα, fall.
πίστις, -εως, ἡ, faith, trust, pledge.
πλεῖστος, -η, -ον, superl. of πολύς.
πλείων, -ον, compar. of πολύς.

πλέω, πλεύσομαι, ἔπλευσα, sail.
πλῆθος, -ους, τό, number, amount, mass, the commons.
πλήν (adv.), except; (prep. +gen.) except.
πλήρης, -ες, full.
πληρόω, fill, man (ships).
πλήσιον (adv.), near; (prep. +gen.) near.
πλοῖον, -ου, τό. ship, boat.
πλοῦς, -οῦ, ὁ, sailing, voyage, course.
ποιέω, make, do, treat.
πολεμέω, make war.
πολέμιος, -α, -ον, hostile; (as noun) enemy.
πόλεμος, -ου, ὁ, war.
πολιορκέω, besiege; blockade.
πολιορκία, -ας, ἡ, siege, blockade.
πόλις, -εως, ἡ, city, state.
πολλάκις, (adv.), often.
πολλῷ (adv.), by much, by far.
πολύ (adv.), much, considerably.
πολυπραγμονέω, be busy, take trouble, meddle.
πολύς, πολλή, πολύ, much, many.
πονήρως (adv.), badly, wickedly.
πορεύω, make to go, convey; (mid. and pass.) march, journey.
πόρρω (adv.), forwards.
πόρρωθεν (adv.), from afar.
ποταμός, -οῦ, ὁ, river.
πρᾶγμα, -ατος, τό, affair, matter, thing; (pl.) circumstances, state affairs, trouble.
πράττω, do, perform, manage.
πρεσβευτής, -οῦ, ὁ, ambassador (for pl., πρέσβεις is used).
πρέσβυς, -εως, ὁ, old man; (pl.) ambassadors.
πρίν (adv.), before; (conj.) before, until.

πρό (*prep.* +*gen.*), before.

προ-βάλλω, put forward; (*mid.*) impeach.

προβολή, -ῆς, ἡ, impeachment.

προ-βουλεύω, deliberate beforehand, pass a preliminary decree.

προ-δίδωμι, give, pay in advance, betray.

προ-ηγορέω, act as spokesman, speak for.

προθυμία, -ας, ἡ, readiness, willingness.

πρόθυμος, -ον, ready, willing, eager.

προ-ίστημι, set before; (*pass. and intrans.*), be set over, be at the head of.

προ-καλέω (*usually mid.*), challenge, invite, propose.

προ-λέγω, foretell, proclaim, order.

προνομή, -ῆς, ἡ, foraging, foray.

πρόξενος, -ου, ὁ, state guest, state friend (*equivalent to consul*).

προ-πίνω, προπίομαι, προύπιον, drink one's health.

πρός (*prep.* +*acc.*), to, towards, against, with a view to; (+*gen.*) from; (+*dat.*) at, near, in addition to.

πρόσ-ειμι (εἶμι, go), advance, approach, attack.

προσ-καλέω, call, summon; (*mid.*) summon, bring into court.

προσ-οφείλω, owe in addition.

προσ-πίπτω, fall upon, attack.

προσ-πλέω, sail towards.

προσ-τάττω, order, command.

προσ-τίθημι, put to, add.

προσ-φέρω, bring to.

προτεραῖος, -α, -ον, previous.

προτεραία, -ας, ἡ, the day before.

πρότερον (*adv.*) before, previously.

πρότερος, -α, ον, earlier, former.

προ-τίθημι, place before, add to.

πρῶτος, -η, -ον, first; τὸ πρῶτον, in the first place.

πρύτανις, -εως, ὁ, president, chairman.

πυνθάνομαι, πεύσομαι, ἐπυθόμην, πέπυσμαι, learn.

πῦρ, πυρός, τό, fire; πυρά, τά, watch fires.

ρ

ῥίπτω, throw, throw away.

σ

σελήνη, -ης, ἡ, moon.

σημαίνω, σημανῶ, ἐσήμηνα, show, point out, give a signal.

σίτιον, -ου, τό (*usually in pl.*), food, rations.

σῖτος, -ου, ὁ (*pl.*, σῖτα, τά), corn, food, provisions.

σιωπάω, be silent.

σκεδάννυμι, σκεδῶ, ἐσκέδασα, ἐσκεδάσθην, ἐσκέδασμαι, scatter.

σκοπέω, σκέψομαι, ἐσκεψάμην, ἔσκεμμαι, look, look for, watch, consider.

σκότος, -ου, ὁ, darkness.

σπένδομαι, make a truce.

σπουδαῖος, -α, -ον, serious, eager, good.

στάδιον, -ου, τό (*pl.*, στάδια *or* στάδιοι), stade, 600 Greek or 606¾ English feet.

στάσις, -εως, ἡ, party strife, faction, sedition.

στερέω, deprive.

στόμα, -ατος, τό, mouth.

στράτευμα, -ατος, τό, army.

στρατηγέω, be general, be in command of (+*gen.*).

στρατηγία, -as, ἡ, command, office of general.

στρατηγός, -οῦ, ὁ, general.

στρατία, -as, ἡ, army, expedition.

στρατιώτης, -ου, ὁ, soldier.

στρατιῶτις, -ιδος (fem. adj.), with ναῦς, troopship, transport.

στρατοπεδεύω, encamp (also in mid).

στρατόπεδον, -ου, τό, camp, army.

συγγενής, -ές, akin; (as noun) kinsman, relative.

συγ-γράφω, compose, draw up a motion.

συγ-καλέω, call together, convene.

συλ-λέγω, bring together, collect; (pass.) assemble.

συμ-βουλεύω, advise.

συμ-μαχέω, be an ally, be in alliance with (+ dat.).

συμμαχίς, -ιδος (fem. adj.), allied.

σύμμαχος, -ον, allied; (as noun) ally.

συμπάρ-ειμι (εἶμι, go), march along with.

συμ-πέμπω, send along with.

συμ-πλέω, sail along with.

συμ-φέρω, bring together, contribute; (impers.) συμφέρει, it is of use, expedient.

συμφορά, -ᾶς, ἡ, chance, misfortune.

σύν (prep. + dat.), with, with the aid of.

συν-αθροίζω, gather together, assemble.

σύν-ειμι (εἰμί, be), be with (+ dat.).

συνεπ-αινέω, join in approving, consent.

συνθήκη, -ης, ἡ, agreement, compact, treaty (esp. in pl.).

σύνθημα, -ατος, τό, signal, password, sign.

συν-ίημι, understand.

συν-ίστημι, put together, combine; (pass. and intrans.) stand together, band together.

συν-ορμίζω, anchor together.

συν-τάττω, draw up together.

συν-τίθημι, put together, construct; (mid.) agree.

σφαλερός, -ά, -όν, dangerous.

σφεῖς, σφῶν (reflex. pron.), themselves.

σώζω, σώσω, ἔσωσα, σέσωκα, ἐσώθην, σέσωσμαι, save, preserve; (pass.) come safe to.

σῶμα, -ατος, τό, body.

σῶς, σῶν, safe.

σωτηρία, -as, ἡ, safety.

τ

τάλαντον, -ου, τό, talent; (worth 60 minas).

ταξίαρχος, -ου, ὁ, commander of a τάξις or body of troops—commander.

τάξις, -εως, ἡ, rank, battle order, body of troops, position.

ταράττω, stir up, trouble, confuse.

τάττω, draw up, arrange, appoint, fix.

ταύτῃ (adv.), in this way, here.

ταχέως (adv.), quickly.

τάχιστος, -η, ον (superl. of ταχύς).

ταχύς, -εῖα, -ύ, swift, fast.

τε (conj.), and; τε ... τε ..., or τε ... καὶ, ... both ... and.

τειχίζω, build a wall, fortify.

τειχομαχέω, fight walls, besiege.

τεῖχος, -ους, τό, wall, fortification; (in pl. sometimes = castle).

τειχύδριον, -ου, τό, small fort.

τέταρτος, -η, -ον, fourth.

τετταράκοντα, forty.

τέτταρες, -α, four.
τεῦχος, -ους, τό, vessel, barrel.
τέως (adv.), for a time.
τίθημι, θήσω, ἔθηκα, τέθηκα, ἐτέθην, place.
τιμωρέω, avenge; (mid.) take vengeance on.
τις, τι (indef. pron. and adj.), some one, some, a.
τίς, τί (interrog. pron. and adj.), who? what?; τί, why?
τοιόσδε, τοιάδε, τοιόνδε, such as ths, such.
τοιοῦτος, τοιαύτη, τοιοῦτο(ν), such.
τολμάω, dare, have the courage.
τότε (adv.), then.
τοὔμπαλιν (adv. =τὸ ἔμπαλιν), backwards, opposite.
τρεῖς, τρία, three.
τρέπω, turn, put to flight; (mid.) turn oneself.
τρέφω, nourish, maintain.
τριάκοντα, thirty.
τριήραρχος, -ου, ὁ, captain of a trireme (at Athens, the one whose public service it was to equip a trireme).
τριήρης, -ους, ἡ, trireme (see Intro. §4).
τρίτος, -η, -ον, third.
τριώβολον, -ου, τό, three-obol piece, half-drachma.
τρόπαιον, -ου, τό, trophy.
τρόπος, -ου, ὁ, way, manner.
τροφή, -ῆς, ἡ, food, provisions.
τυγχάνω, τεύξομαι, ἔτυχον, τετύχηκα, hit, light upon, meet (+gen.); happen.

υ

ὕβρις, -εως, ἡ, insolence, presumption.

ὕδωρ, ὕδατος, τό, water, rain.
ὕλη, -ης, ἡ, wood, timber.
ὑμεῖς, -ῶν (pron.), you (pl.).
ὑπέρ (prep. +acc.), over, beyond; (+gen.) over, on behalf of.
ὑπ-έχω, undergo, supply; λόγον ὑπέχειν, render account.
ὑπ-ηρετέω, serve, minister to.
ὑπό (prep. +acc.), under (towards); (+gen.) by (personal agent); by means of; (+dat.) under, close to.
ὑπ-όμνυμι, -ομοῦμαι, -ώμοσα (usually mid.) make an objection on oath.
ὑστεραῖος, -α, -ον, next; ἡ ὑστεραία, next day.
ὕστερον, afterwards.
ὕω (usually 3rd sing. only), it rains.

φ

φαίνω, φανῶ, ἔφηνα, πέφηνα (intrans.), ἐφάνην, show; (mid. and pass.) be shown, be manifestly, (+part.) appear (+infin.).
φάσκω, say, allege.
φέρω, οἴσω, ἤνεγκον, ἐνήνοχα, ἠνέχθην, ἐνήνεγμαι, bear, bring, lead (of roads), πονήρως φερόμενος, having an evil reputation.
φεύγω, φεύξομαι, ἔφυγον, πέφυγα, flee, flee from, be in exile.
φημί, φήσω, ἔφην, say; (part.) φάμενος.
φθάνω, φθάσω or φθήσομαι, ἔφθασα or ἔφθην, anticipate, do first (+part.).
φίλος, -η, -ον, beloved, dear; (as noun) friend.
φιλοτιμέομαι, be ambitious, pride oneself on.

φοβέω, frighten; (*mid. and pass.*) fear, be afraid.

φοιτάω, go to and fro, go repeatedly, frequent.

φοίτησις, -εως, ἡ, repeated going, visiting.

φράζω, point out, declare.

φυγάς, -άδος, ὁ, runaway, fugitive, exile.

φυγή, -ῆς, ἡ, flight, exile.

φυλακή, ῆς, ἡ, guard, garrison.

φύλαξ, -ακος, ὁ, guard.

χ

χαλεπῶς (*adv.*), hardly, with difficulty, angrily; χαλεπῶς ἔχειν, be angry.

χαρίζομαι, do favour to, gratify.

χειμών, -ῶνος, ὁ, winter, storm.

χείρ, χειρός, ἡ, hand.

χεῖρον, (*adv.*), worse.

χίλιοι, -αι, -α, a thousand.

χράομαι, use, experience, deal with (+*dat.*).

χρή (*impers.*), it is necessary.

χρῆμα, -ατος, τό, thing (*pl.*) money.

χρηστέον, one must use.

χρόνος, -ου, ὁ, time.

χρυσοῦς, -ῆ, -οῦν, golden.

χρώς, χρωτός, ὁ, skin; (*special dat.*) ἐν χρῷ, to the skin.

χώρα, -ας, ἡ, country, land.

χωρίον, -ου, τό, place, spot, district.

ψ

ψεύδομαι, lie, say falsely.

ψηφίζομαι, vote, vote for, carry by vote.

ψήφισμα, -ατος, τό, decree.

ψῆφος, -ου, ἡ, vote.

ψιλός, ή, όν, bare, light-armed; (*as noun*) light-armed troops.

ω

ὧδε (*adv.*), thus.

ὠνέομαι, buy.

ὥρα, -ας, ἡ, season, hour, fruits of the season.

ὡς (*adv.*), how, as; (*conj.*) as, when, that, in order that, so that.

ὥσπερ (*adv.*), just as.

ὥστε (*conj.*), so that.

ADDENDA

προσπληρόω, fill up, complete (a number), man and equip more (ships).

πρῷρα, -ας, prow, forepart of a ship.